Time-Limited Existential Therapy

Time-Limited Existential Therapy

The Wheel of Existence

Second Edition

Alison Strasser
With Freddie Strasser

WILEY Blackwell

This second edition first published 2022
© 2022 John Wiley & Sons Ltd

Edition History
John Wiley & Sons Ltd (1e, 1997)

All rights reserved. No part of this publication may be reproduced, stored in a retrieval system, or transmitted, in any form or by any means, electronic, mechanical, photocopying, recording or otherwise, except as permitted by law. Advice on how to obtain permission to reuse material from this title is available at http://www.wiley.com/go/permissions.

The right of Alison Strasser to be identified as the author of this work has been asserted in accordance with law.

Registered Offices
John Wiley & Sons, Inc., 111 River Street, Hoboken, NJ 07030, USA
John Wiley & Sons Ltd, The Atrium, Southern Gate, Chichester, West Sussex, PO19 8SQ, UK

Editorial Office
The Atrium, Southern Gate, Chichester, West Sussex, PO19 8SQ, UK

For details of our global editorial offices, customer services, and more information about Wiley products visit us at www.wiley.com.

Wiley also publishes its books in a variety of electronic formats and by print-on-demand. Some content that appears in standard print versions of this book may not be available in other formats.

Limit of Liability/Disclaimer of Warranty
The contents of this work are intended to further general scientific research, understanding, and discussion only and are not intended and should not be relied upon as recommending or promoting scientific method, diagnosis, or treatment by physicians for any particular patient. In view of ongoing research, equipment modifications, changes in governmental regulations, and the constant flow of information relating to the use of medicines, equipment, and devices, the reader is urged to review and evaluate the information provided in the package insert or instructions for each medicine, equipment, or device for, among other things, any changes in the instructions or indication of usage and for added warnings and precautions. While the publisher and authors have used their best efforts in preparing this work, they make no representations or warranties with respect to the accuracy or completeness of the contents of this work and specifically disclaim all warranties, including without limitation any implied warranties of merchantability or fitness for a particular purpose. No warranty may be created or extended by sales representatives, written sales materials or promotional statements for this work. The fact that an organization, website, or product is referred to in this work as a citation and/or potential source of further information does not mean that the publisher and authors endorse the information or services the organization, website, or product may provide or recommendations it may make. This work is sold with the understanding that the publisher is not engaged in rendering professional services. The advice and strategies contained herein may not be suitable for your situation. You should consult with a specialist where appropriate. Further, readers should be aware that websites listed in this work may have changed or disappeared between when this work was written and when it is read. Neither the publisher nor authors shall be liable for any loss of profit or any other commercial damages, including but not limited to special, incidental, consequential, or other damages.

Library of Congress Cataloging-in-Publication Data

Names: Strasser, Alison, author. | Strasser, Freddie, author.
Title: Time-limited existential therapy : the wheel of existence / Alison
   Strasser with Freddie Strasser
Other titles: Existential time-limited therapy.
Description: Second edition. | Hoboken, NJ : Wiley-Blackwell, 2022. |
   Revision of: Existential time-limited therapy / Freddie Strasser and
   Alison Strasser. 1997. | Includes bibliographical references and index.
Identifiers: LCCN 2021043976 (print) | LCCN 2021043977 (ebook) | ISBN
   9781118713716 (paperback) | ISBN 9781118713686 (adobe pdf) | ISBN
   9781118713709 (epub)
Subjects: LCSH: Existential psychotherapy. | Brief psychotherapy.
Classification: LCC RC489.E93 S77 2022(print) | LCC RC489.E93(ebook) |
   DDC 616.89/147–dc23
LC record available at https://lccn.loc.gov/2021043976
LC ebook record available at https://lccn.loc.gov/2021043977

Cover Design: Wiley
Cover Image: © Dody Strasser, RBA

Set in 9.5/12.5pt STIXTwoText by Straive, Pondicherry, India

10 9 8 7 6 5 4 3 2 1

Freddie Strasser (1924–2008)

This book is dedicated to my dad, Freddie Strasser, whose wisdom, innovation, and vision, whose passion for the time-limited modular approach, and whose appetite for wheels of every description laid the foundational ideas upon which this book is based.

Thank you for remaining steadfastly by my side as this second edition took shape and for your unswerving belief.

Your Hungarian charm and infectious smile will continue to ripple in all those who have been touched by your irrepressible spirit.

Contents

Foreword *ix*
Preface *xi*
Acknowledgements *xvii*
About the Author *xviii*

Part I *1*

1 **Existential and Phenomonological Philosophies and the Wheel of Existence** *3*

2 **Core of the Wheel: Time and Self** *14*

3 **Time in Therapy: The Principal Concepts of Existential Time-Limited Therapy** *20*

4 **Approaches to Time-Limited Therapy** *30*

Part II *39*

Layers and Leaves: Ontologicals and Ontics *41*

The Ontological Layer: Universalising *43*

5 **The Ontological 'Givens'** *44*

Stepping Through the Ontic Leaves: Individualising *54*

Contents

6   Working with The Phenomenological Process   *56*

7   Establishing Safety   *73*

8   Discovering Anxiety   *81*

9   Revealing the Relationship   *93*

10 Exploring the Four Worlds   *104*

11 Clarifying the Worldview   *112*

12 Working with Paradox and Polarities   *123*

13 Identifying Choices and Meaning   *132*

14 Integrating Mind and Body   *141*

15 Understanding Authenticity   *147*

Afterword: COVID-19   *156*

References   *162*

Index   *168*

Foreword

All therapy, de facto, is time limited and has a beginning and an end. In this it is very much like human existence. The more we allow ourselves to be aware of the limits of life, the defter we get at using the space and time available to us. It is like this with therapy too: the more we approach it with awareness of its limits and boundaries, the sharper becomes its lens, allowing us to throw a clear light on a person's difficulties whilst illuminating their possibilities. Time, here too, is of the essence, as it leads us naturally from our memory-laden past, through our present predicaments, towards a future purpose and destination. Throughout the pages of this book our journey in time points the way towards progress, meaning, and understanding.

When Freddie Strasser and his daughter Alison Strasser co-authored their book on time-limited therapy at the end of the 1990s, they had both relatively recently completed their existential training (with me), but had already shown themselves to be prime contributors to the existential approach. In that earlier book I recognised many of the ingredients I had introduced them to, though they had been mixed and prepared in a new way, providing a fresh and original take on existential therapy that foregrounded the important theme of the time-limited nature of our profession.

In this new volume, Alison Strasser has remixed the themes, elegantly updating her vision of time-limited work, displaying her maturity of thought and her professionalism. Here we find a broader spectrum, a more coherent narrative, and a much more sure-footed account of time-limited existential therapy. This is now a clear and carefully worked out guide demonstrating to existential therapists how they can concretely apply these ideas to their everyday practice with their clients. This is a book by a seasoned and talented therapist, who has not only seen hundreds of clients over the intervening decades, but who has created a thriving existential training institute of her own, in Sydney, Australia, and who has taught and supervised many hundreds of trainees over the years.

The experience jumps off the page and is continuously in evidence through the intertwining of theoretical concepts and practical application. There are many vignettes, whose storylines are engaging whilst highlighting the points that matter. There are great summaries of relevant philosophical ideas and of salient practitioners' work. There are also plenty of original contributions, culminating in a brand-new 'wheel of existence', which will speak to existential therapists worldwide.

Alison Strasser has boldly taken up the challenge of revising and reviving a highly successful book, which she wrote together with her late father. Having had the immense pleasure of knowing and working with Freddie Strasser myself, I have no doubt that he would have smiled proudly upon this feat of daughterly pluck and accomplishment. The book will give his own reputation a new lease of life, thus cheating time and death itself in the nicest possible way. Many new readers will now benefit from their joint ideas, and previous readers will note how these ideas have thrived and blossomed, through Alison's work, over the years. The book is a true testimony to the ripening of life with the passing of time. It will be appreciated on many continents.

Emmy van Deurzen

Preface

The only man who behaved sensibly was my tailor: he took my measure anew every time he saw me, while all the rest went on with their old measurements and expected them to fit me.

George Bernard Shaw, *Man and Superman* (1905)

The first edition of this book, *Existential Time Limited Therapy: The Wheel of Existence* (Strasser & Strasser, 1997), co-authored by my father, Freddie Strasser, and me, paved a pathway to describing how existential therapy offers an effective approach to brief therapy where 'it was the certainty of the ending that was identified as the most influential distinguishing factor' (Lamont, 2012, p. 172). We proposed that time itself is the 'tool' that facilitates awareness and the potential for change.

One of the original aims of the first edition was to convey existential philosophy as a vehicle for common sense. Neither my father nor I saw ourselves as experts in existential philosophy; however, we were both stimulated by how the integration of existential and phenomenological philosophies added alternative perspectives and ways of understanding people that related to their concrete living in the world rather than being limited to a psychological perspective. As is probably true for most existential practitioners, we saw ourselves as existential-oriented therapists, signifying that we are informed by numerous ideas and approaches that build on our own personal experiences.

In the first edition, we presented the modular approach where the client was offered 12 sessions with the first 10 sessions as consecutive and the final 2 sessions spread a month apart. A subsequent module of 12 sessions could be discussed and implemented depending on the client's particular circumstances. Indeed, the discussion itself about continuing or not is one of the hidden gems of this approach in that some clients are adamant about wishing to continue or not. Such responses tend to relate to, and reveal, clients' attitudes towards themselves and to relationships in general.

In conjunction with the development of the time-limited modular approach, the first edition introduced two Wheels of Existence: Structure and Process wheels. This was a novel way of understanding existential philosophy and brought to existential psychotherapy a structure, albeit fluid, to delineate the aspects of existential theory and its application to psychotherapy practice. Since existential philosophy is not used overtly with clients but creates the backdrop or framework to inform how the therapist listens, how questions are framed, and how inferences and connections are drawn, the wheels provided an interrelational map. The various components provide a schema for understanding how the different elements of existential philosophy are integrated into the whole experience.

In the years following the publication of the first edition, my father and I lived in different countries, followed different pathways, and diverged in our interests but still continued with our weekly conversations. I began exploring supervision and devised a wheel to encompass the existential ideas that emerged from my doctoral research. My father became fascinated with mediation and also created a series of wheels to further enhance his ideas and to show the existential connections retained in this mediation framework. He developed the ideas along with Paul Randolph (a barrister) into the Alternative Dispute Resolution. Interestingly, although two wheels were introduced in the first edition, very soon only one wheel emerged in each of our individual work.

In 2007, when writing a presentation for the Australasian Existential Society, my father and I developed yet another version of the wheel that united our ideas combining our developing thoughts. And we realised that veiled within the original text was the germ of an idea that, as life is time limited, similarly every psychotherapy session, every group of sessions however contracted, has its limitations of time (Strasser & Strasser, 1997, p. 4). This we understood as reflective of the need to be time *aware*, irrespective of modality or length of sessions. We had every intention of developing these ideas further into a second edition of time-limited therapy.

However, the time-limited nature of life assaulted my own sense of certainty and predictability with the unexpected and untimely death of my father, forcing me to confront the finitude of his life, taking the wind out of my sails, and leaving me to honour the legacy and continue our work.

When, some years later, Emmy van Deurzen proposed the idea of my writing the second edition on my own, I felt excited to continue my father's work. I had accessed his ideas about paradox on his computer and discovered some of his case studies. I knew how we would have written this book together, as we had done previously. I would now write to honour his work; I would write as a tribute to him.

Several months on, however, I was still struggling to gather my thoughts and put together any words related to time-limited therapy. I was derailed by my wish to write my own thoughts, worried that I'd be unable to do so on my own and fearing offending the existential community. Without my father there was no buffer, and yet I wanted to have my voice heard; I was stuck in my own paradox.

This struggle continued until one of my friends insightfully asked me *why* I was writing. I realised that my intentions were more duty bound than personally motivated. It seemed that my attempts at writing had been in 'bad faith'.[i] Of course I'd be finding it hard!

This has not been an easy journey. In time, I began to appreciate that, as the Bible claims, 'What has been will be again, what has been done will be done again; there is nothing new under the sun' (Ecclesiastes 1:9), that no ideas are new, only that our understanding of concepts evolves with our experiences and our ability to challenge and experiment with them. Even if I present what I believe are new ideas in this book, they have evolved from what has been co-created with others, from my many and varied teachers, mentors, colleagues, friends, adversaries, and, of course, my father.

Since the publication of first edition, many other authors and existential practitioners have written about their work and their understanding and integration of existential philosophy. There is a second and possibly even third generation of writers that are widening and also integrating other frameworks and modalities into the space of existential practice. There is the focusing world of Eugene Gendlin (1978) as integrated by such authors as Greg Madison (2010); the Buddhist mindfulness approach as integrated by such authors as Khong (2013) and Nanda (2009); the continuation of Frankl's (1963) logotherapy with the work of Alfred Längle (2015); as well as the humanists such as Kirk Schneider (Schneider & Krug, 2010) and Mick Cooper (Cooper & Mearns, 2005) who have shown how the humanistic tradition is also existential in nature. Research shows that existential therapy is as valid an approach as any other therapy (Correia, Cooper, & Berdondini, 2014). There is a group of therapists, the New Existentialists (Hoffman, 2015), who no longer adhere to the 'doom and gloom' perspective that is often associated with French existentialist writing, focusing instead on a positive interpretation of the philosophy and its application. Indeed, we now read about joy and hope, meaning and purpose as an existential tension to their opposites of sadness and despair, meaninglessness and aloneness and about how we can live our life more fully through self-examination and taking more responsibility for our life journey. And my own perspective continues to shift and modify as I undertake further reading, add my own daily experience of working with clients, supervisees, students, colleagues, and am challenged and inspired by the vagaries of life in all its complexities.

I returned to writing this second edition, deciding to put my father firmly up 'in the attic' and to give myself the option of choosing consciously when and how to invite him in.

Simultaneously, I realised that my compulsion to complete this task on my own was driven my childhood determination to prove my worth; this contributed to my stuckness. By staying with the anxiety of my stuckness, I began to understand that to ask for help was not a negation of my independence but potentially a shift towards something new and exciting. And so I chose to ask for help. Jo Silbert has been a friend and fellow therapist for many years. Through her love of language, she shifted into writing and editing articles and books on psychotherapy. With her help, this second edition began to take shape.

My first decision was to consolidate the two Wheels of Existence into one wheel. This new wheel combines the ideas from the original wheels and simultaneously allows for the integration of the philosophical ideas and the essential processes involved in existential practice. Broadly, the Wheel in this edition brings together the concept that our practice is phenomenological while maintaining the existential philosophy as the backdrop that informs our listening, questions, and reflections.

In this second edition, I will expand on the concept of time-aware therapy to reveal that all therapy can be viewed as time limited and discuss the various possibilities of using a time-aware approach in practice to reveal how time can be used as an effective stratagem to enhance and highlight some of the existential human concerns. So, while the modular approach still remains valid, its ideas are transferable to all therapies.

Therapy as time limited fits snugly into an existential perspective in that, in its very essence, therapy mirrors life in all its openings and closures, beginnings and endings, with its final culmination in death. These beginnings and endings of life range from the small and everyday – our waking up in the morning and going to sleep at night, starting and finishing a new project, beginning a new friendship and saying goodbye to others – to the more significant beginning of our birth and ending of our death. We are all being carried forward towards death, a *being-unto-death* as described by Heidegger (1962). The manner of our approach to how we tackle or manage these beginnings, endings, openings and closures in therapy can mimic how we negotiate life. Hence, the significance of time is tangible in every session.

Time is also implicit in therapy, though usually unspoken, unless either the client or therapist is taking a break, or the end of therapy is nigh. There are numerous theories and approaches to addressing and grasping the meaning of breaks; yet working explicitly with temporality as an existential given gives a richness to time in all its complexity for both the therapist and client to work with.

I tend to work with clients with no fixed end to their therapy, or what is usually defined as open-ended. This is partly due to my original training and also my own preference for working with clients over a longer period. The relationship that is at the crux of existential therapy ebbs and flow over a longer period and builds on an in-depthness that doesn't always have time to develop within the brief therapy scenario. I build in an ending process so that when it is time for the client to finish, we negotiate a series of sessions before the final closure. This manner of ending brings out many of the advantages of the time-limited modular approach and the benefits for some clients of working over a longer time period. Later, I discovered that this was similar to Otto Rank's (1929) concept of time-limited therapy that I shall return to in Chapter 3. As so cogently described by a supervisee who closed her practice using this 'time-aware and time-limited' approach, 'working with the ending was like a dream come true; my clients took up their own baton and truly worked in earnest'.

Yalom (2008) writes about explicitly alluding to death in every session; I propose that our relationship to time is an expansive way of calling attention to endings that might include our relationship to our physical death but is inclusive of all the other beginnings and endings that occur in life. Every session has a start and finish, every day has its morning and night, every job has an induction and termination, and all relationships begin and end. By calling attention to this reality, it allows for the possibility of working with all the intrinsic anxieties, paradoxes, and vulnerabilities highlighted in the modular approach explored in the first edition.

The proposal to bring time-limited awareness to all therapy is about recognising that contextual working situations are diverse, that our circumstances differ, and that, as therapists, we have personal preferences. My work as a supervisor has privileged me with insights into the gamut of the many and varied circumstances, contexts and experiences of my supervisees: therapists and supervisors in private practice; practitioners that work in agencies with a fixed number of client sessions varying from 6 weeks to 6 months; those that permit additional sessions; those that require clients to be referred elsewhere after the maximum sessions are complete. These insights have highlighted how we all need to find our own path, our own voice as therapists. Working with the idea of time and its limitations has its own flexibility and can be used and worked with as seen fit and appropriate by each individual.

In some obvious, some subtle ways, this second edition was in its conception – both during and as soon as the first edition was put to bed – reflecting the notion that speaks directly to one of the existential ideas that time is in constant flow with no beginning or ending. This might appear to be in direct opposition to time-limited therapy which honours the idea that time is limited, thus highlighting another existential 'given' that life is peppered with paradoxes. This second edition is an opportunity to extend the original ideas around time in therapy to include a broader spectrum of practitioners and clients. There are many advantages to shorter-term therapy and there are other benefits to working in a more long-term way. The requirements of the client, the orientation of the therapist or the specific agency rules are all taken into account when contracting with the client. In all of these circumstances, understanding and working with time as an explicit theme can alter the flavour of the therapy. Case studies and client vignettes will be used throughout the book to illustrate and to breathe life into what is often turgid or difficult language to understand. This edition includes new case studies and vignettes as well as those from the original book, namely, 'Lynn', one of the studies written by my father which was pivotal in the development of the time-limited modular approach. In this second edition, all of the other case studies are composites and representative of being human.

Much has changed since our writing of the first edition, including my understanding and working definition of time-limited therapy. My own practice as a therapist, supervisor, coach, and trainer continues to inform my understanding and interpretation of existential philosophy. I am indebted to my clients, supervisees, and colleagues for the questions they ask and their inherent courage to question not only themselves but me in any of these roles and positions.

The second edition is written to be inclusive of many of the ideas that were important to my father. I decided to use the pronoun 'I' rather than define which ideas and client stories were his and which were mine. This decision was part of my personal process of finding my voice and recognising my father's influence.

Finally, as my father had, and still has, enormous influence on who I have become and on the way I think and experience life, this second edition honours both his contribution to the world of existential practice as a therapist, coach, and mediator and the immense impact he had on defining the modular time-limited approach. His framework still works and continues to be enormously useful.

Note

[1] A term used by Jean Paul Sartre (1958) to describe a form of self-deception and avoidance of one's freedom.

Acknowledgements

I'm deeply grateful to my sisters Carolyn and Yvonne, to my step-daughter Sacha Woodburn, to all my family, friends and colleagues who have supported me in my much longer than anticipated journey in completing this second edition.

I have travelled around the world, sat at many kitchen tables with my trusted laptop and both written, revised, and conversed with my wonderful friends and family; in particular, the tables I remember with warmth are with Nari and Lucia Ghandhi in London, Frank and Sara Megginson in Monaco and other beautiful settings, Peggy Hankey in Seyssel, France, Sal Flynn in Byron Bay, Margalit Barnea in Portugal, Jo and Alex Fok in Tasmania, and Annie Buchner in our COVID-bound holidays in New South Wales, Australia, and a big thank you to Leanda Elliott and Joyce Morgan for their wise counsel and unswerving friendship.

I thank my colleagues who never erred from the firm belief that I would finally hand in the manuscript. In particular, Emmy van Deurzen, Ernesto Spinelli, Greg Madison in the UK and, closer to home, Adam McLean and Lyn Gamwell.

And I thank all my clients and supervisees who inadvertently provided the backdrop and clarity to the existential themes that I was writing about, including their myriad of responses to time, and to Maria Clark for sharing her time and her rich case studies for inclusion in this book.

I acknowledge the calm and insightful support of Jo Silbert who stepped in after the first draft as my editor and mentor; together we cut and dissected chapters, pages, and ideas and shaped them into the current coherent creation.

Finally, my thanks go to my husband Rob Woodburn who was a surreptitious existential thinker, only revealing later in our relationship that he had studied existential philosophy as an undergraduate. As a writer, he patiently read and edited the first draft of this book, asking awkward but poignant and useful questions. The two most significant men in my life, Rob and my father, Freddy both died within 10 years of each other, handing over the baton to my humble and nervous hands.

About the Author

Alison Strasser DProf (Psychotherapy & Counselling), MA, BA Hons

Alison is a practising psychotherapist, coach, and supervisor. She is also an educator with a passion for imparting how existential themes can be integrated into every therapeutic approach. She was instrumental in creating the existential curriculum for many counselling and psychotherapy trainings in Australia and founded Centre for Existential Practice in 2008. Her doctorate focused on the process of supervision, work that led to a framework for supervisor training, now a major component of CEP's annual programme.

Part I

1

Existential and Phenomonological Philosophies and the Wheel of Existence

> *My freedom will be so much the greater and more meaningful the more narrowly I limit my field of action and ... surround myself with obstacles ... The more constraints one imposes, the more one frees one's self of the chains that shackle the spirit.*
> Igor Stravinski, *Poetics of Music in the Form of Six Lessons* (1970)

Existentialism and Phenomenology Overview

Existentialism and phenomenology are different and yet complementary philosophies that attempt to understand what it means to be human. In simple terms, existentialism focuses on human existence, reflecting on the issues of what it is to be human, while phenomenology concerns itself with how human beings subjectively interpret their existence. These philosophies stem not from a traditional, objective, rational, scientific focus or impetus but from an examination of how humans understand themselves in the midst of their lived experience.

The word 'existence' has its roots in the Latin word *ex-istere* – translated variously as 'to stand out', 'to emerge', 'to proceed forward in a continuous process'.

Rollo May, the distinguished American protagonist of existential philosophy, defined this existential approach to understanding the human condition in his book *The Discovery of Being*:

> For the very essence of this approach is that it seeks to analyse and portray the human being – whether in art or literature or philosophy or psychology – on a level which undercuts the old dilemma of materialism versus

idealism. Existentialism, in short, is the endeavour to understand man[1] by cutting below the cleavage between subject and object that has bedevilled Western thought and science since shortly after the Renaissance. (May, 1983, p. 49)

Existential philosophy is concerned with the science of being – with ontology (Gk *ontos*, 'being'). It examines the attitudes we adopt towards being and what we can do about it. Existential philosophy observes that each individual makes his or her own unique pathway in the world, that each of us will experience our own existence in our own distinctive manner. Simultaneously, each individual exists in a relational or co-constituted mode to others and to the world. In other words, as soon as we exist we are inexorably connected to other people, objects and even ideas.

Kierkegaard, the grandfather of existentialist philosophy, explored the anxiety and aloneness humans experience as they struggle in their attempts to find their own truth, their personal freedom, against the backdrop of the 'shoulds' and 'oughts' that life inevitably demands. Heidegger pertinently asked, 'What is it to be human?' and spent his life's work defining and redefining both his questions and answers, emerging with the concept that humans are inextricably connected to the world, are perpetually in a state of 'being-in-this-world', known as *Dasein* (Heidegger, 1962). Similarly, we are always 'comporting' or choosing how we act in the world at the same time as the world interacts with us.

Many people associate existential philosophy with complicated ideas and a leaning towards pessimism. They hear words such as 'death', 'isolation', and 'meaninglessness', without realising that these concepts form only a part of a richer and more complex whole. It is just as significant, for example, to explore hope as it is to examine despair. The polarity of existential themes creates the constant tension between life and death, meaning and meaninglessness, isolation and relationship. Existence is about understanding and living within these constant tensions.

Phenomenology, on the other hand, concerns itself with subjectivity, with how human beings interpret things to themselves (Husserl, 1977) as opposed to the natural science framework that seeks to find objective truth. The importance of phenomenological exploration is that it excludes this objective reality and instead seeks a subjective explanation of the individual's relationships with objects, others, and his or her sense of being.

The Wheel of Existence

The Wheel is used as a diagrammatic representation of the interplay between key existential and phenomenological concepts and as a philosophical attitude when working with clients. It is versatile framework in that it can be used as a specific

Existential and Phenomonological Philosophies | 5

Diagram: Wheel of Existence

Outer ring (ontological givens): ENGAGEMENT, RELATIONSHIP, FACTICITY, UNCERTAINTY, TEMPORALITY, MOOD, FREEDOM, EMBODIMENT, MORTALITY, ANXIETY, CHOICE

Inner leaves (ontic layer): Exploring the Four Worlds; Working with Paradox & Polarities; Understanding Authenticity; Integrating Mind and Body; Discovering Anxiety; Revealing the Relationship; Clarifying the Worldview; Identifying Choices and Meaning; Establishing Safety; Working with the Phenomenological Process

Core: TIME, Secure Self, Insecure Self

Source: Alison Strasser

structure for teaching but also creates a background frame that can be drawn upon when reflecting upon a client either in the session or later in supervision.

In brief, the Wheel's outer layer depicts existential or 'ontological' phenomena, the concerns or 'givens' common to all human beings universally.

Radiating from the fulcrum of the Wheel is the next layer, a series of 10 segments or 'leaves', which together constitute the essence of individual experience and their attitudes or relationship to the ontological 'givens'. These leaves are referred to as the 'ontic' layer and give credence to a subjective and personal 'ontic' experience which differs with each individual and which more closely resembles the concerns of phenomenology.

The self, which can be considered to be in a constant state of flux, shifting between one's experiences of security and insecurity, occupies the outer section of the core.

At the core of the Wheel of Existence is time, an existential given that permeates all our lives from birth to death and beyond.

The Wheel is a schema for understanding how the different rudiments of existential philosophy are integrated into a whole; it seeks to show how all the above elements both interact with and influence each other, all contributing to the individual's experience of being-in-the-world and to our worldview. The structure of the Wheel highlights the existential–phenomenological hypothesis that all issues always interconnect and express themselves throughout all facets of individuals' relationships with the world. As such, the Wheel parallels existential philosophy in viewing the human being as a unified entity rather than split into divisions of mind, thoughts, body, and emotions. It follows that what a client focuses on at any point in time will be connected to many of their other concerns, thus paralleling phenomenology. In keeping with this thinking, the following chapters in which these elements or 'leaves' are described do not necessarily follow the clockwise or even anticlockwise direction of the Wheel.

Of course, the paradox is that existentialism by its very nature cannot provide anybody with a framework that guarantees safeguards or stability. If the Wheel is taken too literally or becomes too technical or rule driven, it can easily become counterproductive. Using a loose but clearly defined structure, however, can also highlight the uncertainties of being thrown into this world and the certainty of leaving it, which Deurzen confirms: 'Although an existential approach [to psychotherapy] is essentially non-technological, I also believe that one needs some methods, some parameters, some framework, in order to retain one's independence and clarity of thinking' (1988, p. 6).

Universalising: The Ontological Layer

The outer edge of the Wheel of Existence in the diagram encompasses what are known as the ontological or existential concerns of existence. These 'ontological' characteristics are the elements of being human that are common to all humankind. They are aspects of being human that we cannot change; they are an intrinsic feature to all humans. In existential terminology, they are called 'givens' or 'universals', meaning facts that we are either born with or encounter during life. Residing in the background of our everyday living, I think about these ontological givens as the relentless 'hum'. These 'hums' are constant and move in and out of immediate awareness as events in life unfold. For Heidegger, this ontological aspect is at the heart of his understanding that certain aspects are manifest and inescapable and are the nature of being human (Heidegger, 1962).

Various authors have described a range of different themes of existence as 'ontological'. The concerns chosen within this Wheel, and discussed below, are the ontological givens that arise most commonly in my current work and will be discussed in detail in Chapter 5. Other therapists might focus on other givens that give credence to their practice.

The Ontological Givens
- *Relationship* in the ontological sense describes how a human being is always in a state of relationship not only to others but also to oneself and to the overall

culture and environment. This understanding does not make any statements about the quality or the nature of the relationship but simply states the fact that relatedness reveals itself in the relationship.
- *Facticity* relates to the limiting factors that we cannot fundamentally change including certain features such as our own genetic makeup, our psychological profile, our cultural heritage, and our social world.
- *Uncertainty* and inconsistency is a feature of life that we cannot avoid and which the world imposes upon us.
- *Temporality* 'is the name of the way in which Time exists in human existence' (Warnock, 1970, p. 62) and nobody can escape from the idea that life is moulded by our finitude, that we are only transitory beings on this planet.
- *Mood* is the way we are 'attuned' to the world and describes how we are both experiencing and responding to our existence. 'A mood assails us. It comes neither from "without" nor from "within", but arises from *Being-in-the-world*, as a way of that being' (Heidegger, 1962, p. 136).
- *Freedom* is connected to responsibility in that humans are not determined by external factors which are certain, but, within the limitations of existence, are free to create their own responses to living.
- *Embodiment* denotes the concept that humans are both physical and non-physical, are both mind and body. A body–mind experience will both shape and be shaped by our interactions in the world. 'We are both subject and object, where the subject *is* his body, his world, and his situation, by a sort of exchange' (Merleau-Ponty, 1964, p. 72), where the object is subsumed into this exchange.
- *Mortality* is our constant awareness that we are moving towards death, the end of our known life. It is our ultimate limitation, which cannot be removed, only denied or engaged with.
- *Anxiety* is that state that is constantly in our background revealing to us both our discomfort and excitements generated by aspects of being human, such as the choices that seem out of our control, our moving towards death and our freedom.
- *Choice* is inevitable in that we are constantly making choices, even when we are unaware of doing so. Even choosing not to choose is a choice.
- *Engagement* (or Action) is how we choose to participate with the world, whether fully, partially, half-heartedly, with passion and so on. Closely linked to our values, the idea of engagement also indicates our authenticity.

This ontological space is where we share a common resonance with other human beings about all that it is to be human, in a world that is replete with both limitations and possibilities.

It is also the space that, as therapists, we share with our clients in that we too are travelling on a journey through life's tribulations, despairs and joys, in search of meaning within lives without inherent meaning and living with all of life's paradoxes – all part of the process of coming to terms with living and dying. Ontology also facilitates our mutual caring or concern, which Heidegger describes as interconnectedness with others.

In practice, our exploration of ontological concerns merely reflects our innate sense of what it is to be a human being and doesn't describe our personal response to these givens. Although the 'givens' described above may be immutable, the way we perceive or interpret them and the attitude we take towards them is always open to interpretation.

Individualising: Our Ontic Responses

Inasmuch as the ontological layer is made up of elements that are common to all humankind, the ontic layer reflects our individualised and cultural responses to the universal 'givens'.

Hans Cohn succinctly describes the distinction between ontological and ontic thus:

> an ontological enquiry explores those aspects of Being which are 'given' and inescapable . . . But each of us responds differently to these 'givens' of Being and creates his or her specific world within the all-encompassing world of Being. An exploration of the specific way in which each of us is in the world is called 'ontic'. (Cohn, 1997, p. 13)

The inner segments of the wheel that circle the central core are known as our ontic responses and give flavour and depth to our personal being-in-the-world. They both reveal our personal relationship to each of the ontological givens and represent the various different processes used during therapy. Each of these segments indicates both the descriptive 'how' of working within the phenomenological process and the 'what' of the existential theme under inquiry.

Each of the individual segments within this central part of the wheel illustrates the principal themes that indicate our lived experience, our individual responses to the immutable, ontological givens described above. The segments are both separate and flow into each other, framing the exploration that occurs with clients. As with all themes, they can be explored individually but are not seen in isolation as everything is connected to the whole of an individual's experience.

The Ontic 'Leaves'
- *Working with the phenomenological process* is the relational approach to being-with the client. The process itself creates a space for both client and therapist to

notice, watch, re-ascribe or 'open up' to their experience, allowing other choices to come to the fore. (Chapter 6)
- *Establishing safety.* As a counter to the experience of uncertainty, we all attempt to create safety. In psychotherapy, contracting and establishing the frame helps to create an artifice of safety. (Chapter 7)
- *Discovering anxiety* is to acknowledge life's uncertainties and inconsistencies, revealing that anxiety is a *sine qua non* of existence. 'We must all face inevitable death, groundlessness, isolation and meaninglessness' (Yalom, 1980, p. 485). Therapy helps us to explore how we live with and respond to our anxiety. (Chapter 8)
- *Revealing the relationship* refers to the notion that we are always in relationship – a significant component of existential therapy. (Chapter 9)
- *Exploring the four worlds* is the recognition that we experience and live simultaneously in our physical, social, private and spiritual worlds, an experience which is integrated into our being-in-the-world. (Chapter 10)
- *Clarifying the worldview* is the exploration of our personal principles and the process of gaining understanding about how our belief and value systems both serve and give us our freedom yet have the potential to become entrenched or 'sedimented', filtering and often limiting our worldview. (Chapter 11)
- *Working with paradox and polarities* acknowledges that everything has an opposite, which is often contradictory. Not everything is reconcilable, neither is it necessary to be so. This recognition opens us to an understanding that opposites can coexist and thus to a more comprehensive and complex both/and experience rather than the more common either/or position of splitting our experience into reality-polarising opposites. (Chapter 12)
- *Identifying choices and meaning* is at the heart of existential philosophy, which contends that we are forever making choices in light of the meaning we ascribe to the situations in which we find ourselves. (Chapter 13)
- *Integrating mind and body* is a view that expresses how we experience life through our thinking and our emotions and simultaneously sense through our bodies. (Chapter 14)
- *Understanding authenticity* helps connect an individual to their story in a manner that reveals not only their personal world but also how they affect and influence others and the environment in which they exist (Chapter 15)

Each of the individual segments within this central part of the wheel illustrates the principal themes that indicate our lived experience, our individual responses to the immutable, ontological givens described above; they will be explored in Section 2. The segments are both separate and flow into each other, framing the exploration that occurs with clients. As with all themes, they can be explored individually but are not seen in isolation as everything is connected to the whole of an individual's experience.

There is always a flow, an interaction between the ontological and ontic where the ontic is our personal and individual response and our actions to 'the concrete, changing and practical aspects of existence' (van Deurzen & Adams, 2011, p. 154). Mortality, for example, is an existential given but each of us will respond differently to the idea of death, whether it be to live in eternal fear of its imminence, to live every day as if it were our last, to live in denial of death or to live with awareness of the inevitability of death and to manage the impact on us of this awareness.

Core of the Wheel: Time and Self

In this updated version of the Wheel of Existence, the segments revolve around time and the ever-changing self at its centre.

Time as one of the tenets of existence refers to how we engage with or experience time and temporality within the dimensions of the past, present and future. Time is the way we relate to the hum of temporality and all of the other ontological givens.

Time itself is a social and personal construct that furnishes us comfortably with a convenient structure as we move from birth to death, from day through to night, from experience to experience, from moment to moment. Time is closely connected with endings of all types, evoking different reactions, and is worked with and addressed in therapy.

The Wheel of Existence figuratively demonstrates how time can be deemed as the centre of our existence. It informs every micro-second of our waking and sleeping life and influences the way we understand our past, live in the present and imagine the future. Time both influences and interacts with all the elements that constitute the 'expression of the sum total of our particular way of being with or engaging in the world' (Strasser, 1999, p. 11).

Time also interacts with and influences our concept of our self. In existential terms, we are continually reacting to what is happening to and around us and we are constantly making moment-to-moment passive and active choices. The self continually shifts and flows between feeling worthy and secure and inferior, doubtful and insecure, as we find ourselves in relationship with the ontological givens and our ontic responses. The self is thus in constant flux.

Time and the self will be explored further in Chapter 2.

The Principle of Interconnectedness

The World and I are within each other.
        Maurice Merleau-Ponty, *The Phenomenology of Perception* (1962)

The dividing lines between the sections of the Wheel are blurred or intentionally indistinct to denote the interconnectedness of human concerns or 'givens', the overlap of our ontic reactions and the interplay of our ontic reactions with the ontological givens that underpin them. Both the universal existential givens and our individual responses to these universal givens are incorporated into the Wheel of Existence so as to signify the interplay between the two.

Husserl (1977) coined the term 'intentionality' from his questioning of the Cartesian mind/body and subject/object dichotomy. In opposition to Descartes's maxim *I think, therefore I am*, Husserl developed a theory that refutes the separation of our thinking self from being and advocates that our thoughts, body, emotions, and our connection to the external world, our environment, are always in relationship with each other and woven into the fabric of our existence. He argued that we are constantly interpreting and consequently constructing meaning out of every situation, every thought, every interaction from our own unique standpoint. He suggested, furthermore, that our understanding of everything is experienced in our consciousness in its entirety and is inextricably joined to our perceptions of them.

Simply put, if I am conscious, I am always aware of something. When I become aware of my anger, for example, I might also notice that my anger is directed towards something or someone (Husserl, 1977). If we take this further, I might become aware that my anger is pulsing through my body and memories may begin to arise of situations where I might have felt similarly. Simultaneously, sadness, fear or other emotions might emerge where a possible link to some particular sense of uncertainty might be felt as I begin to reflect on my lack of control and feeling of unease.

This interconnectedness amongst all things in our experience includes the interrelationship between the two philosophies of existentialism and phenomenology and, as the Wheel demonstrates, the relationship between ontological givens, ontic reactions, time, and self – and, indeed, the therapist's resonance with client's subjective experience. All of these interconnections will be explored more fully in Section 2.

Application to Psychotherapy

> *Existential therapy is a process of truth finding. It aims to help people to disentangle their lives and generate clarity. It addresses all-important issues directly and encourages a person to reconnect with a strong sense of personal direction. Careful attention is paid to both the universal and the particular aspects of a person's existence in order to understand the relationships and tensions between them . . . People learn to live deliberately rather than by default.*
>
> Emmy van Deurzen, 1997, p. 236

Integral to working existentially with clients is the integration of other applied or practical philosophies such as dialectics, Socratic dialogue and hermeneutics – but probably most importantly, that of phenomenology. As an applied philosophy, this is sometimes described as the phenomenological method of investigation, a term which sounds somewhat aloof but is, in fact, the opposite in that the interweaving elements bring forth a relational connection between therapist and client. Simply put, a phenomenological attitude helps us become aware of our judgements and biases, fostering a spirit of wonder, curiosity, and admiration as we 'tune' in, and attempt to understand our client's worldview.

Tucked within the layer of leaves are the nuggets of existential and phenomenological practice that bring forth both the phenomenological, relational process and the various approaches to working with the existential themes as they arise within the therapy. This will be explored more fully explored in Chapter 6.

As time in general underpins the way we relate to the hum of temporality and to all of the other ontological givens, so time and temporality are a constant in the therapeutic relationship. Every beginning has an end and every ending opens itself to new beginnings. Time, the effects of ending and the temporal aspects of each session are intrinsic elements within any therapy. The manner in which both the client and therapist are able to negotiate the continuum between the start and the closure of each session as well as the overall journey is worthy of its own exploration and understanding. Sometimes endings are difficult to talk about and sometimes they reveal themselves at the most opportune moments.

There are as many different ways of considering and integrating the existential perspective into psychotherapy practice as there are readers of the texts. Overall, and possibly most importantly, the existential therapist is asked to make their own interpretation of the philosophy and integrate this personal perspective into their practice. We all bring our individual essence to the practice of the philosophy.

The following example demonstrates how the Wheel may be employed to explore a client's experience and how the segments of the Wheel interact to shape his reality:

> Serge at 5'5" (*facticity*) believed that he was tall (*worldview*) and acted accordingly, ensuring that he maintained his tall stature by standing on the balls of his feet (*physical dimension*). Serge was also attracted to tall women (*revealing the relationship*). His personality stood out as someone who was funny, curious and intelligent with a largesse that was attractive to others (*mind and body*). He suffered a rude awakening, when looking at a video, and was shocked to realise that he was the smallest of his peers (*authenticity*). He wasn't as tall as he imagined. This led us to explore (*phenomenological process*) his desire to stand out (*choices and meaning*) in all his four worlds.

> Serge, as the youngest of four boys with a dominant father, had felt insignificant and small (*polarity*). As the youngest and smallest he hated being petted and patronised, which made him feel small and demoralised (*anxiety*). He wanted to be treated as big and substantial like his brothers and developed a personality to match this desire (*meaning and choice*). If he felt he made the wrong decision about anything (*self-esteem*) he would feel wracked with guilt and felt small and inconsequential. Serge was always proudly prompt as this related to his desire to be seen by others (*interpersonal relationship*) as reliable and responsible (*worldview*). However, he avoided the future, agonised about decisions (*time*) as this related to change and uncertainty.

The Wheel of Existence provides a frame or background integrating the philosophy of existentialism with the practice of phenomenology: existentialism, in its quest for understanding and asking the questions about our living and dying; and phenomenology, in its pursuit to more fully comprehend the client's worldview within all the vagaries and tensions that we encounter as human beings.

For all its advantages, with the Wheel providing a structure and an anchor and as an invaluable tool in therapy, it is still a metaphorical not literal representation of the existential themes that arise within our humanness. It offers a guide for the therapist to listen, to note and even discover the connections within the Wheel, as it pertains to an individual's unique experience, providing a structure for reflections and possible interventions.

Note

1 Gender-specific references in this and other quoted material appear in the original text.

2

Core of the Wheel: Time and Self

> *Time is the substance I am made of. Time is a river which sweeps me along, but I am the river; it is a tiger which destroys me, but I am the tiger; it is a fire which consumes me, but I am the fire.*
> Jorge Luis Borges, *Labyrinths: Selected Stories and Other Writings* (1964)

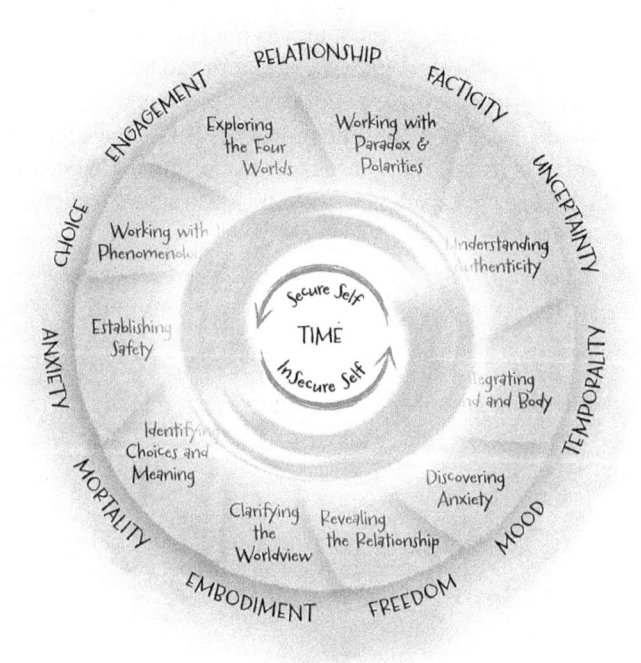

Source: Alison Strasser

Time-Limited Existential Therapy: The Wheel of Existence, Second Edition. Alison Strasser.
© 2022 John Wiley & Sons Ltd. Published 2022 by John Wiley & Sons Ltd.

This chapter begins our journey through the layers, levels, sections, and segments of the Wheel. We start with the idea of time and its interaction with the ever-changing self as the centre of our existence, symbolically represented by time and the self being located at the centre of the Wheel.

Time as the Centre of Existence

It might be obvious that we are always in time. To live authentically, however, requires that we cultivate a particular awareness of time and its impact on us. Time cannot be considered as a solo and separate concept but as intertwined with all aspects of our being, as depicted in the Wheel of Existence. For instance, both the past and future are imbued with meaning, and events in our present life impact our understanding of our past and our future direction.

Time can be considered in more than one way. Time as cosmological is essentially infinite. It is one of the unbounded 'hums' of existence. It is not mine to possess; it is its own master. In contrast, time as an entity is a social construction, formulated by society to give meaning and structure to the passage of time. In our Western world, this construction is dominated by the Gregorian calendar, the chronological clock dominated by Greenwich Mean Time and a perception that the general direction of time flows out from the past towards the present and into the future.

For Heidegger, time was more than an entity; he considered it to be ontological (1962), contending that time is constant, it is eternal, it is cosmological and is intrinsic to being. He argued that time is not linear 'but the past is carried along by a present that is already anticipating the future' (Cohn, 1997, p. 14). He suggests that to live authentically requires a particular awareness of time, an understanding that being *is* time, that to be is to exist temporally on this path between birth and death (Heidegger, 1962).

Beginnings are intertwined with endings. The end can be the finality associated with our physical death as well as the end of specific events such as the end of a psychotherapy session, leaving home, or quitting a job – and, of course, the ending that occurs in all relationships. This is in keeping with Heidegger's idea that humans are thrown into the world in time and are always projected forward to the ultimate end (1962). Time is related to our innate sense of the unity of past, present, and future; it is finite, coming to an end with our death, and is also infinite in that it continues without us after we die.

Existential philosophers distinguish between the experience of living in time – which is what is known as 'thought time' (Binswanger, 1963, p. 301), that is, the way we are aware of time – and 'lived' time, which refers to our inner knowingness of the passing of time and which includes the idea of coming into being and disappearing from being. This view of time gives a different perspective to the concept of living in the Now where our recollections and view of the past can only be viewed from our present time. Time never stands still but is influenced by and continually moves between the past, present, and future dimensions. We are always in present time, but our present time is constructed out of our present perspective of the past and the future. We only access any past event, both its content and feeling, from our present perspective. So, there is no actual past, only our current interpretation of that past. And the same for the future, in that we are only imagining a future from our current emotional and physical perspective.

For Heidegger, time is the fundamental aspect of his thesis in that we each live our lives within temporality, with the inner knowing that our lives on this planet will end. Heidegger notes this as our 'Being-towards-death' that is future directed and is unique to humans who have this capacity to transcend the present and project towards the future that is full of possibilities. 'Every moment of change connects us to our death anxiety' (Spinelli, 2016, p. 135), implying that living in time is not static but embedded in change. This gives us the movement of forward living with the possibility of both hope and despair.

Time is concrete, in that we can be aware of every ticking second, grounded in the reality that the ticking is forever moving forward towards an end. Simultaneously, we can experience time as disappearing, stopping, and sometimes eternally stretched. Time is also elusive in that the past, in its detail, gets forgotten and remembered in fragments and bite-size packages, and the future is only in our imagination, yet we often act as if it is true. 'We measure everything in life by change and the passing of time, because we ourselves are always no longer what we were and not yet what we will be' (van Deurzen, 2014).

Time lies within us whatever we do or whatever happens to us. As an ontological given, time is common to us all as human beings and provides an overarching and all-encompassing mantle over our existence.

The location of time at the core of the Wheel is indicative of how time and temporality are essential to our existence and, as described in this book, a central component in our therapeutic work. Time is at the forefront of our minds as we formulate the contract with our clients and how we negotiate time both within and between sessions. It includes how we experience time in general and within the therapeutic frame.

On each occasion that we sit down with a client we are at a beginning. We have no idea what the client has experienced during the week and how they will re-enter the relationship in that beginning moment. The same is true for how the client is experiencing their entry into the therapeutic space and their meeting the therapist.

Each time we begin a session with a client, we are also facing an end.

> Maggie's husband, after years of feeling confined by marriage and children, had decided he wanted time to find and relate to himself. Although Maggie could intellectually understand his wishes and could even contemplate her own freedom, she inwardly collapsed so that her previous routines of going to work and spending time with the children became onerous and overwhelming. Our sessions would commence with a rundown of her weekly events but soon moved to a never-ending assortment of her thoughts. Every week, I could feel her horror when the session was over and she would have to step out of my room into the world on her own. When she was by herself, she found peace by taking a bath. The same was true when she had someone else's total attention, someone who was absorbed in her world. In both these spaces she felt connected, so the hum of time was peaceful; it receded into the background. Conversely, in the face of endings, in having to negotiate with others or in having to think about the future, her anxiety welled up, causing her to imagine an uneasy future which would be continually disrupted; the hum of time became foregrounded and disturbing.

Self: The Secure–Insecure Continuum

In the core of the existential Wheel, residing alongside time is the self. The phenomenological understanding of time as a shifting space applies equally to our notion of self. As is the case with time, the self is not a constant to be located but is elusive, as it shifts from moment to moment in response to each situation as it arises. As is the case with time, the self interacts with all the sections of the Wheel.

In this version of the Wheel of Existence, time is placed at the core to denote its centrality of meaning and intent. Circling the inner core of time is the secure and insecure self that, in existential terms, signifies a self that is not fixed or entity-like but instead is seen as self-in-process that continually reinterprets and reshapes its identity from the multiplicity of derived experiences.

There is no concept of a self on its own; the self is totally relational and exists only in intimate connection with other people, concepts, ideas and the world around us. Not only do we come into relationship with others, but they also come into relationship with us. They are witnessed by us and we are witnessed by them, and so for Heidegger, 'we can never encounter only [ourselves]' (1962, p. 274). 'We cannot . . . understand – or make sense of human beings – our selves included – on their own or in isolation, but always and only in and through their inter-relational context'.

This idea of a 'relational self' is highlighted when we think about how the responses of others affect our sense of who we are, our self-esteem. Other people's opinions – or more realistically, our perception of other people's opinions – are at the forefront of how we view ourselves. Since we are so connected with others our sense of self is intimately tied to the other, often creating a kind of roller coaster reaction in terms of our self-esteem. We can move from momentary feelings of exhilaration to dismay within a flash should someone inadvertently or purposely say something negative about us.

In this relational understanding of the self, our self-concept is also intricately entwined with our value system. We continually assess how well we are conforming to our acquired and desired values that then translate into our self-esteem. For example, if we value being accepted and liked, we will need to please others to feel acceptable to ourselves. When our strategy works and we receive approval, we feel flattered and good about ourselves. The opposite is also true: when we desire approval, and our attempts to gain it by striving to please others don't work and instead we feel someone's dislike or disapproval, our self-esteem may take a battering.

Furthermore, we can also say that our self-concept is linked not only to values but also to our perception of safety, our notions of time and temporality as well as with all the other sections represented on the existential Wheel.

The idea of the 'relational self' embraces the phenomenological principle that we are continually defining, constructing and reinterpreting who we are as we meet life in our moment-to-moment interactions. We move continually from feeling secure, good, okay or hopeful to being thrown into disarray and feeling insecure, bad, not okay and pessimistic. In the core of the Wheel, the arrows denote a continual flow representing this ever-shifting sense of self from secure to insecure.

This understanding of self as a fluid experience that oscillates and shifts is quite different to that often proffered by the humanist thinkers with their belief that the self is within us, can be found and is to some extent 'static'. It is remarkable how this prevailing attitude towards the 'real', 'fixed' or genuine self is embraced in the minds of the general public.

The notion of 'plasticity' can be borrowed from neuroscience to support the existential understanding of a fluid self. Sometimes referred to as neuroplasticity, the 'plastic' brain is a term used to describe the brain's ability to change and adapt as a result of experience. We continually create new synaptic connections, which in essence is how we form new memories. As we tell and retell our stories, we add and subtract from our narrative, creating something new in each retelling.

When we take into account the notion of the 'plastic' self – the self that is not stagnant, that is ever changing – the process of therapy itself becomes flexible. It is not only the client that changes; the idea of the 'plastic self' also signifies the importance of the therapist retaining an open mind and not becoming fixed on how the client's sense of self might be at any given moment. This availability of the therapist to stay present to the client's shifting experiences of self in turn assists the therapist to not fix or label and to facilitate the client's own journey to finding their path.

> Returning to Maggie, she was more secure and could easily self-reflect when in a space where she felt uninterrupted and connected, such as during our sessions. When having to negotiate other people's requests both at work and with her husband, or having to navigate her children's concerns, she became highly anxious and self-critical. In theory, Maggie knew that she was capable and a warm, loving person, but often this 'self' was replaced by a 'self' that believed she must be lacking if her husband and sometimes her children didn't want to be with her. In those moments, in contrast to these other connected, relational moments, she lacked self-esteem.

Maggie illustrates the connection between time and her relationship to her ever-changing self. As we journey through the remaining layers, levels, sections and segments of the Wheel, we will add to our understanding of the vast interconnectivity of our living in the world, our existence.

3

Time in Therapy: The Principal Concepts of Existential Time-Limited Therapy

Time: I can live it. I can give it. But I cannot hold it, even for a second, as it slips swiftly, invisibly through my fingers, away into the past.
Erik Craig, 'The human and the hidden' (2008)

Traditionally, existentialists have eschewed both the concept of an external structure and specific tools, believing that by remaining open to whatever emerges in the therapeutic relationship brings an openness and aliveness, which is the very essence of freedom. The facticity of our birth and death, however, means we are born into a finite, temporal structure. Life is about learning to live within this imposed structure of birth and death. This existential given of life and death, or beginnings and endings, imparts a structure, limit or boundary to everything we do including the therapeutic encounter. However, as much as existentialists wish to remove structure from their practice, this would seem an impossible task. This conundrum additionally demonstrates that paradox is implicit in existential philosophy.

Time, as previously described, is a constant hum, usually implicit and often not explored in therapy sessions. We may talk about how quickly a session went but tend not to describe how this affected us or what it meant that time passed quickly. Time is also implicit in how sessions are structured and how client and therapist handle the prescribed time frame. One client might leave their most important point to the last minute while another will rush straight into their burning issue. The point of interest is to ponder together on how these different presentations relate to their relationship with the time limits of the session and how it might intersect with the Wheel's other ontological givens and the ontic leaves of their experience.

Time is a significant catalyst for change, so working with time brings the themes of therapy into sharper focus. Once there is knowledge of an end, of a limit to the process of therapy, a different atmosphere is instantly created. The constant presence of the ending elicits its own pressures for both the client and the therapist; it heightens the anxieties and intensifies the tension for the client, who may expect to be 'cured', and for the therapist, who wishes to help.

There are many different ways of working within the time-limited methodology; these will be discussed in Chapter 4. In this chapter we explore the theme of time within the context of psychotherapy and examine how a greater awareness of this theme, and even working with time more explicitly, can bring a client's issues to the fore.

The role of time in psychotherapy is the main thesis of this book. As such, I suggest that a deeper understanding of the role of time in psychotherapy will catapult the client's (and therapist's) insight into how they live within their own temporality. In working with the paradigm of time itself, where time is used explicitly as a focus of reflection within the framework created by beginnings and endings, openings and closings, we begin to note that all therapies can be perceived and worked with from the perspective of time.

The knowledge that therapy will end is always implicit right from the beginning, whether the contract is for brief or longer-term therapy. How clients approach beginnings and endings and how the therapist responds to these strategies will immeasurably influence the middle stages of therapy. In the first few sessions, clients usually reveal something of their relationship to endings, and the meaning that endings hold for them.

The middle stages of most therapy situations are usually not defined unless review sessions are built into the contract. In a brief time-limited setting, the middle section is relatively short with the end clearly defined. As such, the ending is overtly influencing the process. With longer-term therapy, on the other hand, the middle stage is undefined and ongoing, so the end or the ending is less overt – it will occur sometime in the future but is still implicit.

The single most important distinguishing feature of a time-limited therapy approach is that the *limitation of time itself* becomes a therapeutic tool and is connected to all the givens of existence. This book elaborates on the first edition by extending the concept of *time-limited* to *all* therapeutic encounters irrespective of the duration.

The way in which clients negotiate the timing of their sessions is an indication of their relationship to time, of how they assimilate their therapy into life and of their therapeutic issues. The client who will only schedule sessions at the end of the day or at the weekend may be making a distinction between their work hours, where they are required to be emotionally present, and their personal or non-work time, where they might be giving themselves permission to be in emotional confusion; in this case, time is being cut up and allocated to different modes of being. The client who likes consistency, requiring the same ongoing weekly time slot without wishing to contemplate an end, may be comforted by a sense of certainty, an inner knowing that their therapist is located in the same position at the same time, offering a sense of safety against the vagaries of life and the uncertainty of death; in this case, time becomes a way of self-regulating the anxiety generated by uncertainty. The client who wants therapy to conclude as quickly as possible may want strategies to ward off the anxieties that life throws up, believing that if one runs through life swiftly, one might avoid any reflection on the nastiness of life including the emotions that endings might bring up; here, time is being managed as an avoidance strategy.

Additionally, the manner in which clients direct the therapeutic hour and how they manage the days in between are all worthy of attention, as these behaviours often act as interesting benchmarks for exploration. Most clients have an awareness of time passing in the session and have strategies for using this to their personal advantage.

> When Martin was in crisis, he was always on time, would pay his invoice quickly and was eager to get work done in the session. The intensity that occurred in the sessions gave him the sense of responsibility, that he was doing something positive about his issue rather than not doing anything and it helped him ward off the dread that something else might happen if he wasn't vigilant to time. As the crisis became less urgent, he became tardy, arriving late and frequently changing the times of his weekly appointment. Now, time didn't seem so empty as he was able to fill it with more positive activities, giving his previous troubled sense of self a necessary boost in esteem.

Each therapist, each client and every relationship will reveal its own peculiar and unique process of working relationally with time.

> On the anniversary of her husband's death, Penny had a dream about losing her husband and asking someone else to find him. In the telling, it began to sink in that her husband was truly dead. Yes, Penny knew he had died but at this anniversary juncture she realised that she was beginning to experience her mother's death in a different, more concrete way.
>
> Penny's dream facilitated the conversation around death, time and her expectations of her marriage. Penny had assumed that that relationship was everlasting and that her husband would always be part of her life. At a subliminal level, she admitted that she had known that he was ill and likely to die before her, yet had continued to live as if he would live forever.

Often, it is the therapist who becomes the prompt for talking about the finitude of time:

> After reflecting upon the dream, it became obvious that our relationship was also under scrutiny. Just as Penny had desired her husband's constancy, so did she assume that therapy would just continue, until I broached the possibility of ending. Although Penny was initially quite calm about the prospect of the end of her therapy, her fear that she wouldn't be able to cope on her own soon emerged. Through our work, Penny came to realise that she was alive, that her husband's death didn't kill her and that she was stronger than she had imagined. We completed our sessions within 5 weeks and Penny ended in the knowledge that she would continue to live, albeit differently to how she began.

Existential time-limited therapy exactly mirrors the temporary nature of our existence with its losses and gains, beginning and endings, and the inevitability that life is one of change. All therapy is time-limited and as such can benefit from working with time as an explicit theme. Each session represents a microcosm of our relationship to time and temporality, and how we respond to this reality becomes an intriguing factor worthy of exploration. Time – or rather our relationship to it – is one of the key components or 'tools' for reflection and is considered and talked about from the moment therapy begins.

As therapists, we are working with time and its permutations. Some existential therapists (Yalom, 1980) believe that it is imperative to resolve, accept or learn to live within the parameters of the session or life itself as the defining sense of therapeutic progress. Myself and others (Spinelli, 2007; Strasser, 1999; Deurzen, 2012) understand that it is our response to time in its absolute limitation that is the point for reflection and discussion. As such, there may be no 'cure' to our anxiety about living and dying but rather awareness, an assembly of how time affects us in all its paradoxical complexity. We have to live within the tensions of life anxiety and death anxiety.

Expectations Rather Than Goals

Most time-limited models (De Shazer et al., 2007) use goal setting to create a specific focus with which to work during the stipulated number of sessions. However, the broader notion of working with a client's expectations, desires or even hopes rather than specific goals is more in line with the existential approach. In some ways the language is immaterial; the real significance is in exploring with clients their thoughts, ideas, hopes, and wishes to bring voice to their dilemmas (van Deurzen & Arnold Baker, 2019).

The importance of establishing and clarifying with clients what they anticipate from the process of therapy may bring out both unrealistically high and low expectations. Some clients express their cynicism, while others believe that the therapist will provide the miracle cure. It is important to explore these expectations. The exploration in itself reveals a great deal, including the client's attitude towards others.

Therapists, too, have the opportunity of discussing their expectations, and in so doing, disclosing their perspective and values relating to the therapeutic process. For instance, my preference is to see clients weekly at the start of therapy. This weekly intensity and continuity help to foster my understanding not only of the client's world but also of my responses and reactions to the client. Other therapists prefer fortnightly gaps, perceiving that clients reflect and gain more from the space and time between sessions.

There appears to be a belief that because a time frame may be limited, it is necessary and more feasible to limit the content. Even within the brief frame, no matter which focal concern is chosen, it soon drops into the background as other foci come to the fore. Indeed, time itself is a better theme to bear in mind, as it is a constant throughout the therapy. It is the glue that binds both therapist and client in their journey, revealing attitudes, values, and beliefs across many different avenues of exploration. In any case, keeping the focus broad also highlights the systemic feature that resolution in one area of the client's life will facilitate change in other areas.

Through an exploration of expectations there is an acknowledgement, too, that changes do occur during the life of therapy as they obviously do in life.

Stephen had a fear of flying. He had put his own time limit on therapy as he fully expected to jet around the world without fear within 15 weeks. He also came armed with his own theories, having read many books on the subject of phobias. He appeared to be enjoying the process of exploring, clarifying, and challenging many of his beliefs and behaviours. He also did a great deal of writing in between sessions, where he would clarify his thoughts. But time was ticking away and Stephen, feeling the pressure of this, became angry in the sixth session because he believed he was no closer to getting on his aeroplane. He felt cheated and manipulated by the therapist.

Instead of avoiding Stephen's anger, the rest of the session was devoted to his sense of time, and how he felt when it was out of his control. He began to piece together several instances when time was an important factor. For example, for work he often had to fly to different locations, which would mean getting up early in the morning, working until late and then taking the last

> plane back. It emerged that again he felt cheated because his employers were too penny-pinching to put him up in a hotel overnight. Essentially, he resented having to work under these conditions. Even when he flew to exotic places for holidays, he felt cheated. Holidays were supposed to be fun, but instead he would feel restless and lonely, wondering what he was doing.
>
> Through this exploration, we discovered that the pressure of time, including Stephen's expectations of his therapy and the sense of feeling swindled, were intricately interrelated.

First Sessions and Expectations

The first session with a client is significant in that it is key to how the therapy will proceed. This first session is essentially about contracting. If working within the brief or modular timed-limited frame, the number of sessions is clearly allocated, as will be explained in Chapter 4. Negotiations relate to the frequency, establishment of appointment times, breaks from therapy and therapy setting. The frame is also a safety net for the therapist since this is the place to iterate personal boundaries such as contact outside of session times, confidentiality, use of email, online sessions and text messages, cancellation policies, fee structures, holidays. Apart from delineating the physical space, boundaries are an expression of the therapist's subjective, internal boundaries and are duly noted by the client and translated into what is possible and what is not.

Some therapists use written contracts with their clients and others prefer verbal agreements, but, in all cases, certain specific criteria such as confidentiality and its limits are universal. Although traditionally existential therapy has derided the notion of assessments, the reality is that both the therapist and client are assessing each other, even if informally, from the moment of first contact, if not before. As with all practitioners, the existential therapist may be required to conduct a formal assessment and make informed choices, however, '[t]he accuracy of any diagnosis given is always secondary to the meaning of the diagnosis for the client' (van Deurzen & Adams, 2011, p. 125).

Endings and Expectations

Paradoxically, even in the first session that is all about beginnings, the idea of ending is already in the mind of both therapist and client. The client in the first session will often be wondering about the duration of therapy, whether this is verbalised or not, and the therapist too will be assessing the type of therapy best suited to the client. If time is not discussed as an explicit theme, the concerns and feelings about ending remain either as an unreflected-upon and unrealised topic or as an impediment to the therapeutic flow. This tacit theme may continue throughout with occasional flashes of illumination, such as when the therapist takes a break, or the client misses a session.

In a specified time-limited psychotherapy, the unequivocal end is known from the beginning. There is usually a contract of between three and twelve sessions. If there is an option for a further series of sessions, this option is discussed at the beginning. Ideally, one or two follow-up sessions are included to take place within 4 to 6 weeks after the conclusion of the original course of therapy. Discussing the number of sessions in the first session is of paramount importance. This conversation will bring to the fore both the client's and therapist's expectations of therapy.

Otto Rank (1929) clearly understood that the ending of psychotherapy was an essential phase, introducing the concept of an almost separate and delineated ending. He related endings to fears around life and death, including the anxieties of loss and separation where 'Separation is inevitable, a part of existential reality. Ideological therapies extend indefinitely, searching for some sort of cure' (O'Dowd, 1986, p. 146). Yalom (2008) writes about every session being suited to talking about death since death is unremitting, requiring immediate reflection and integration into life. Similar to death, endings are both real and symbolic in every aspect of our lives and we can all benefit from developing a deeper appreciation of this.

This more explicit approach to time has great resonance for the existential therapist working with clients in a more open-ended or longer-term therapy. When contracting with clients in a time-aware but open-ended approach, the specific end date is necessarily variable.

The more complex question is at what stage of therapy to talk about the end. The short answer is that it is dependent on the client, their presenting issues and how the therapist is responding to their client and those issues. Often clients will raise the topic themselves with questions such as 'how long?' or 'when do I know when it's finished?' Sometimes, the end is talked about in the first session and in other circumstances it may not be raised until later.

I used to rationalise that the ending is in the hands of the client, trusting that they would know when their work was finished. Sometimes this does happen, and we can move seamlessly into a negotiated ending process that might vary from 1 week to 3 months. Even with all the smooth talk about endings, however, there is always the client who confronts us by sending an 'ending text' or who, in the latter part a session, unexpectedly reveals their intention to terminate. Or, when a client 'drifts' away from therapy, client and therapist can become complicit in either not identifying this development or in not bringing therapy to a close. In this silence they can forego the abundance of material that a closing

Principal Concepts of Existential Time-Limited Therapy | 27

session can bring to the fore. It's all too easy to justify why a client is not returning and/or the reasons we do not pursue them. However, this manner of 'drifting' probably has much to reveal about how both client and therapist deal with closures in life in general as well as the specific termination of therapy. Calling a client in for a closing session permits a conversation around endings by client and therapist so that it is assimilated into everyone's understanding of temporality.

Clients may not talk about ending for many and varied reasons: they may be afraid of offending the therapist; they may not be able to imagine life without therapy; they may not want to confront the emotions that endings may bring forth as well as a myriad of other possible scenarios. A conversation around endings, however, can be constructive for both client and therapist. If not raised by the client, in this time-aware approach it is important to talk about endings in the preliminary sessions and establish what an ending signifies for each client.

Therapists too will have a range of reasons to end or not: these might include tentativeness about acknowledging or even knowing the correct time to end since it may be a taboo topic; it may result from personal issues around separation and ending.

> I had assumed, incorrectly, due to past experiences with pregnant clients, that Lara would want to end therapy when she gave birth. I was mistakenly working towards an ending, when Lara started talking about how her husband had agreed to look after the newborn so she could continue.

In any event, for every client that ends therapy, there are potential financial or professional implications for the therapist, such as a personal sense of success or failure that may well contribute towards delaying the inevitable.

Whatever the situation, there is often a point when working towards an end benefits both the client and the therapist. This moment is not always easy to detect or pinpoint and it is made easier if the topic of ending had been introduced as a point for discussion at various intervals when appropriate. Often it is when the sessions become more mundane, less urgent and more routine, where the conversation focuses on events and stories rather than their grasping for meaning or reflecting about themselves and life.

Nevertheless, however much one is prepared, the actual 'end' moment may still be abrupt.

> George initially came to therapy at a crisis point in his life. His business was failing, his family life was dreary and he felt drained and uncreative. His crisis was also precipitated by his parents entering an old age home and his

inability to face up to both his parents' and his own mortality. Indeed, George was so adept at avoiding this topic that it was only much later, when I realised that our sessions had reached that 'checking in' point, that I wondered how much our ongoing therapy related to his innate desire not to end, not to talk about his parents' ageing nor his own growing older and ultimate death.

When I broached the possibility of finishing, it became clear that George had also thought about it but dismissed the possibility out of fear of being left on his own. His trepidation at the thought of ending inspired a conversation around the benefits of integrating endings and closures in a different way into his personal experience. We decided on eight sessions.

George's paralysis around the topic of his ageing parents quickly re-emerged. Our previous sessions had begun to represent the return of his sense of being invigorated and alive, yet as soon as our conversation turned towards his parents, he froze. George was terrified that he might end up as powerless as them, where life controlled him rather than having his own agency. This feeling was similar to his feelings in early sessions when George, in his crisis, had no vitality, little self-worth and an inability to trust his instincts. Our continuing sessions had become a way of warding off his terror of endings. By agreeing to the more finite process of eight sessions, George's issues relating to endings became illuminated, he forced himself to confront his dread and we used the time available for him to understand that although the end was inevitable, it hadn't arrived; he still had his life. He also began to notice that his parents were not as terrified as he had imagined them to be. It was even possible to consider that they were in a different stage of life and were accepting and enjoying their new circumstances.

On a different tangent, after 10 sessions of intense work, Margot talked about ending. I was confused, because from my perspective, I had not anticipated an end at this point in time and thought there was more of her journey to travel. Margot revealed that after reading the first edition of *Existential Time-limited Therapy* (1997), she had assumed that we would be finishing at 12 sessions. On a positive note, this misunderstanding provided us both with a good laugh and led to a conversation about the frailty of being human.

Irrespective of what time, timing, and its various manifestations may mean for us, or what we may think they could mean for our clients, if we become aware of time-related unease on their parts or even similarly notice our own time-related discomfort, it can be therapeutically useful to bring the topic into the conversation to try and find meaning together.

Time is a fundamental notion and the perception of the passage of time always influences therapeutic interactions. The ending will always evoke some kind of emotional response from the client, whether it is expressed as unimportant, as a sense of relief or as a fear of separation. All responses relate back to a client's value system, and their specific habits of confronting the issue of time. As such, whatever the response, it offers a valuable opportunity to explore our clients' internal experiences and to understand them further.

4

Approaches to Time-Limited Therapy

> *That we are, after all, part and parcel of the life process; that we do naturally abhor not only ending but also never ending, that we not only fear change but the unchanging.*
> Jessie Taft, *The Dynamics of Therapy in a Controlled Relationship* (1933)

Traditional psychotherapy tends to be open-ended, without a specified end date, allowing for a broad range of conversations pertaining to the client's world with all its existential themes as they relate to their past, present, and future aspirations. Due to its free-flowing nature, the client has the freedom to process and to reflect on their experience as it is lived in their current time. It tends to have a timeless quality – or rather, time is generally only discussed when time presents as an overt consideration, such as holidays, serious illness or when other interruptions to the sessions occur. If time and the client's relationship to time are not discussed, one of the drawbacks to this open-ended approach is that the therapy itself can lose some of the impetus that occurs when the finality of an ending is foreground. Open-ended psychotherapy can, however, easily incorporate the advantages that an overt focus on the limits of time can bring to shorter therapies.

Time-Limited Therapy

Time-limited psychotherapy as a specific framework tends to be understood as referring to brief or short-term therapy. This is one way of understanding a time-limited approach. On the other hand, since therapy mirrors life, it is useful in therapy to foreground the fact that humans are living with the constant knowledge that life, as we know it, comes to an end. Another fact, similarly, is that the therapeutic relationship will terminate. The acknowledgement of this flow of time within therapy is not only an acknowledgement of this certainty but also allows both the client's and therapist's attitudes to this inevitability to emerge. Hence, working with the prospect of the limit of time and endings is emphasised in this book whether therapy is brief, short-term or open-ended. For this reason, I prefer to think about this approach as *time-aware* therapy.

Open-ended Therapy

As mentioned in the previous chapter, Otto Rank (1929) first described how longer-term therapy is, in fact, also time limited and how he used a fixed number of sessions to process the end and to assimilate any issues around separation and loss. From an existential perspective, the process of ending is negotiated with the client and assigning an agreed number of ending sessions again allows for the knowledge of time and its limitations to arise.

Time and temporality are a constant within the therapeutic relationship. Each session has a beginning and an end, as well as the intervening stretch of time between sessions. As all therapy is time limited, integrating the passage of time and the inevitability of ending into the therapeutic work, it can help to engender a life attitude in clients that is more realistic, more at ease with the life/death, beginning/ending tension that is a shared aspect of being human. These ideas match Heidegger's (1962) philosophy that we only become true to our self by confronting and making meaning of our ultimate finitude.

Depending on the client's sensitivities, the first session is often a good place to talk about time and how the client understands endings. Or this might emerge in the stories they bring about closure, the relationships they've had (both work and personal) and their willingness to leave or to stay in situations beyond their expiry date.

For some, it is uncomfortable to discuss endings, while for others it can be a relief. Irrespective of clients' reactions, these are points of reference that are suggestive of the way they live with both beginnings and endings. An individual's expectations about what may be possible within their personal time frame reflects something of their belief system and helps to illuminate their relationship to time. If we take into consideration that both therapists and clients are affected by time, then the existential approach enables the therapist to challenge this pressure of time and to reflect on what this might reveal within the specific relational dynamic of the client and therapist.

> It was the first time Adrian had talked to anyone about his personal problems. He prided himself on being a private person and believed that he could think himself out of disordered patterns of behaviours. This had worked well until

> his wife began to complain about his anger and how she found it hard to talk to him about what she was unhappy about. Adrian was initially shocked, not realising that his strategies of privately solving problems were inconsistent with his wife's approach. Although Adrian did not find it easy to talk, he revealed in our first session that his father had died from a heart attack when Adrian was 12, following which he had become the 'little man' for his mother and sister.
>
> As we discussed our contract, I also commented that it would be important for us to remain alert to when it would be a good time to end and for him to bear this in mind. Adrian worked diligently in therapy for about 18 months and then began to slow down. After one of my holiday breaks, he malingered for a further 3 weeks before returning. This turned out to the be the ideal moment to talk about finishing. As suggested by Otto Rank, who believed that endings in themselves were a significant component of therapy and for which he would introduce a time-limited termination period to work through client's specific issues related to closures and endings, Adrian and I agreed on a further five sessions to focus openly, and together, on separating and leaving. Indeed, this process illuminated a vulnerability around endings: that finishing his therapy would have felt as if he was abandoning me. We were thus able to work on this old pattern and towards a healthier approach to endings.

In this time-aware and open-ended approach, the same framework is used as other open-ended therapies around regularity of sessions, holiday breaks, and cancellation fees but the end is always held in mind and a structure is created for therapist and client to process the ending together.

Brief Therapy

Generally, brief therapy is known for working within a defined period of time, anywhere from 1 to 25 sessions (averaging 10) to help a person resolve or effectively manage a specific problem or challenge. The existential position is that even when a client presents with an overarching concern, it is unnecessary to focus on only that aspect of their condition since all our issues are interconnected.

Brief therapy, with its mutually agreed-upon, fixed number of sessions, has motivating benefits, especially when the therapist holds the focus of time and ending throughout the sessions. Equally positive is that, by necessity, this fixed-session approach enforces a particular kind of engagement for both therapist and client. The therapist does have to suspend his or her preconceived ideas of what should or should not happen within the time available and has to be aware of their own internal pressure to achieve something in the available time. The client will be responding to their internalised sense of time.

In brief therapy, it is important that the first session clearly delineates the time frame – the number and duration of sessions, the frequency, the cancellation policy, and the process of ending. It is worthwhile to negotiate, if possible, that the final session be spaced a few weeks after the penultimate meeting, allowing the client to integrate and reflect on their progress. A final session a few weeks later provides the space for clients to see their changes and presents the opportunity to reflect on the end or to discuss whether further sessions are required. If clients are given breathing space to apply their learning without recourse to their therapist, they often experience a surprised sense of achievement.

It is common practice for those working with brief approaches to operate within the frame of goal setting. Goals tend to appear as more measurable and therefore in alignment with the current trend towards evidence-based practice. Additionally, on the surface, setting goals would seem the logical sequitur to working within a defined amount of sessions. The argument is that the process of working towards naming goals both brings forth a greater understanding of what is important for the client and sifts out the specific goal that is more attainable in the time available.

As previously mentioned, rather than goals, my preference is to work with client expectations, hopes, and what they envisage from therapy as I believe this offers greater flexibility and permissiveness to the process. It also allows for a conversation to ensure that clients' expectations are reasonable.

All too often I hear the complaint from supervisees that the client is being let down by the system, that there are not enough sessions. It is often helpful to ask, 'not enough sessions for whom?' and the answer often relates to the therapist's personal belief about cure or change or indeed how they are affected by the client's anxiety about ending. The reality is that with continuing reduction in funding, it is often the case that agencies can only offer a fixed and final amount of sessions to their clients. Albeit time limited, for clarity this is better defined as brief therapy. Nevertheless, the reduction in sessions doesn't necessarily mean that clients are being let down. On the contrary, the limitations of time can illuminate the therapeutic issues and, if worked with, can, as described above, be therapeutically useful.

In contrast, for some clients the tension of a short time frame can trigger or set off old patterns of responding to a stressful event and can impede or prevent a useful therapeutic flow occurring. In these cases, the advantages of a longer, relationally driven approach needs to be considered, where the topic of termination is deferred until the client is ready to integrate the succession of ending into their world.

Modular Approach

> Denise completed her 12-week course and her two follow-up sessions. Her initial presenting problem of depression appeared to have dissipated and she had explored various issues in the process, among them a rigid behaviour pattern of optimum control. A few months later, however, she returned to therapy not because of depression but because she had begun to be overwhelmed by anxiety. She said, 'It felt as if the first few months only lifted the lid off the Pandora's Box. Now I need to know where to go with all these feelings and thoughts.'

After a series of clients like Denise it was found that there are occasions when the 12 weeks, plus the two follow-up sessions, prove to be too restrictive; that sometimes one series of sessions could feel incomplete. Hence, a modified approach, with the idea of modular time-limited therapy, was born, giving a more flexible idea to setting the time frame.

The modular approach as developed and described in the first edition of this book (Strasser & Strasser, 1997) consisted of offering clients a fixed number of sessions, initially in a single block, with the potential of further blocks or modules of a similarly fixed amount of sessions; hence the concept of the modular approach to time-limited therapy. It is a version of the brief therapy approach described above that allows for further sessions to be added to the original brief, time-limited contract.

Initially the idea of offering another block of sessions emerged from the initiation in the 1990s of the National Health Service in Britain offering a fixed number of sessions, often with an option of applying for a further series of sessions. Matching the session plans to these organisations, the modular approach also has the possibility of offering clients a further 'module' or series of sessions. Since the concept emerged in the latter half of the last century, out of the cultural change from open-ended to a more structured approach to client work, the intention of the therapist is to work within the agreed-upon time frame. However, adding the idea of 'modular' acknowledges that in some cases it is deemed appropriate and indeed honourable to continue into a second series. Some authors (Lamont, 2012) have argued that this reduces the benefits of working with this specific understanding of 'time limited'. However, if the argument that all therapy is time limited is taken, then it is irrefutable that the benefits will be unmistakeable whether the client is offered one module or two.

As with the brief therapy, the spacing of the last one or two sessions gives the client the opportunity to integrate their understanding. The interval may also reveal the necessity for further sessions. It also mirrors the manner in which some clients approach therapy, accepting that they like to take a break between a module of sessions and adding a further series as they wish. Working constructively with these blocks of time has an inbuilt review process that has been shown to be effective (Bowen & Cooper, 2012).

The common factor between the brief and modular approaches is that the endings are navigated as part and parcel of the therapy, as described previously.

> Viv had three series of modular therapy and is an example of how some people use the specific limitation of sessions to their advantage. The first module focused on how she was going to leave her husband; the second was scheduled as she began to set up her own business; and the third sequence was organised as her children left home. Through the three modules, the theme of loneliness was paramount but each time she integrated another aspect of the complexity of aloneness into her everyday experience.

Often, clients are relieved when the option of a specific number of sessions is offered. The thought of visiting a therapist regularly for an unspecified length of time, possibly years, although comforting to some, may be a daunting, undesirable or unrealistic prospect to others. There are others who may be terrified of clear-cut endings. Separations can become very awkward and using this time-aware approach to ending allows for the process of ending to come to the fore with due reflection, compassion and greater understanding. Indeed, a time-aware approach allows the matter of endings itself to be one of the therapeutic issues worthy of consideration. Shirley's case offers a perfect example.

> The institution where Shirley's therapist worked had offered Shirley only eight sessions with a proviso that, under certain circumstances, further sessions could be granted. She came to therapy outlining a problem of deep depression, insomnia and panic attacks. It transpired that Shirley was a transsexual who had been born a man and had undergone a sex-change operation. She told a story of an extremely unhappy childhood, throughout which she felt that she had been born into the wrong gender. She had been unequivocally convinced that being a woman would bring her total happiness. Although the operation had been a technical success and some of Shirley's peers accepted her new persona, she could not find the complete fulfilment she had hoped for.
>
> Despite her lifelong dream being realised, she descended into a state of suicidal depression. The therapist involved felt overwhelmed and frustrated. It seemed impossible to overcome such an intensive problem in a set number of

> sessions. We explored various possibilities that might prove suitable and effective for both the client and the institution. We arrived at a framework of a module of a further eight sessions followed by two review sessions that we hypothesised would be accepted by the institution. This brought a sense of relief not only to the supervisee and the client but also to the institution that did agree to this structure.

The method of working in modular blocks proved rewarding for everyone involved. As was the case with Shirley, at the end of one module or series of specified number of sessions, some clients may not feel ready to finish, feeling that they are still too tentative to continue their journey on their own. One of the advantages of the modular method is that clients are able to negotiate another series of sessions, which in itself will usually reveal aspects of the client that can be explored and understood as part of the therapy.

Working within this modular frame offers flexibility within the concept of a time-limited approach. It has other benefits in that it can also be used as an assessment period before decisions are made about how the therapy might unfold, and indeed, whether to proceed with the therapy. By taking this assessment period, which might be anywhere from 3 to 12 sessions, as a complete process with a firm beginning and end, both the therapist and client can gain insights from this use of time.

> When Donna arrived, I felt that she was incredibly uncertain about whether any kind of therapy would help her. I was also unsure whether I could develop any empathy for or resonance with her. We agreed upon three sessions followed by a review. Although cautious, by the start of session three she seemed to show signs of using her time constructively for self-reflection and observations about others in her life. She agreed to a further module of six sessions.
>
> Donna's life was structured and busy. She managed her stress by controlling her life, her relationships and her therapy with no leeway to be dependent on anyone, including me, leaving me with a feeling of anger about her control over me.
>
> My supervisor and I explored how I reacted to Donna's control of the sessions, which to some extent explained my initial caution about working with her. I was also curious as to how her desire for control both helped and hindered her in her personal and work relationships. I found that the fixed ending gave Donna and myself a timely process for exploring control and its impact on herself and others in her life, including me. There was never any talk of a further module.

The ability to trust is intrinsic to the entire therapeutic process. It is important that the sense of trust is not marred by an ambivalence that can so easily be created if clients feel they have been left with unresolved issues when a module ends. Therapists who adhere to a strict number of sessions may find themselves in an awkward position, questioning whether to prolong the therapy or allow the client to finish at that point. The modular time-limited approach both eliminates this ambiguity and allays fears of interminable therapy.

Keeping the aspects of time limitation in the foreground intensifies the clients' work on their issues not only during sessions but in between. Furthermore, the gap between one module and another often results in many insights that in turn, as explained earlier, may initiate a change of perception.

Which Time-Limited Approach to Use?

Some clients have a horror of termination; some will force an ending; others create a stop-start approach to therapy. As an existential therapist, there is no necessity for a proscribed demarcation around duration. More importantly, it is how the theme of time unfolds and is negotiated that reveals both the client's and therapist's worldviews and approaches to life and relationships.

It would be pleasing to write explicit instructions for when and how to use each type of time-limited approach, but since this is existential therapy the onus returns to the therapist to make that judgement call in line with the requirements of the client. It is not clear cut and will be influenced by factors such as place of work and authorised number of sessions, personal style and preferences, experience and training as well as the client's story, experience and expectations.

Broadly, the assessment process includes the desire and willingness to remain open and flexible to whatever arises between therapist and client, from moment to moment and session to session. It might include the therapist's preparedness to experiment and courage to deviate from the original agreement if and when appropriate. This might mean interrupting the flow and changing from a modular to open-ended approach or the reverse. Irrespective of any decisions about the approach taken, the specifics of the conversation, the process that emerges between client and therapist is of significance and will ultimately transmute into the contract. Hence if there is a change to the time and nature of the therapeutic sessions then the contract, whether verbal or written, needs to be revisited. In essence, the therapist has to be attuned to the ever-changing nature of the client's ever-evolving sense of self and what they may require to enhance their journey. It requires sensitivity on behalf of the therapist and an element of courage to both notice and articulate what may emerge in the between-ness of the therapist and client as well as their everyday world.

Time is with us at every single point in our existence, it touches us constantly in our waking and our sleeping lives and is both essential and inseparable from the therapeutic process. Time represents so blatantly how we react with either the limitations it imposes on us or the freedom it might give us. In revealing how we each respond to this fact of life, it also reveals our beingness in the world.

Whether working with expectations or goals, or within a short-, medium- or long-term therapy framework, it is important to work with how time is perceived. If the therapist can suspend the desire to pursue goals and the need to cure the client, and instead 'be there' with the client in an interpersonal relationship, then paradoxically this may enable the therapist to create the desired therapeutic atmosphere for the client to evolve a reflective, more aware sense of themselves that brings forth actions that are more thoughtful and less reactive.

By placing time at the forefront of our existential givens, this book is offering the opinion that open-ended time-limited, brief and modular therapy are all various options to taking a more constructive approach to working with time.

Part II

Layers and Leaves: Ontologicals and Ontics

There is not one big cosmic meaning for all; there is only the meaning we each give to our life, an individual meaning, an individual plot, like an individual novel, a book for each person.
  Anaïs Nin, *The Diary of Anaïs Nin, Vol. 1: 1931–1934* (1969)

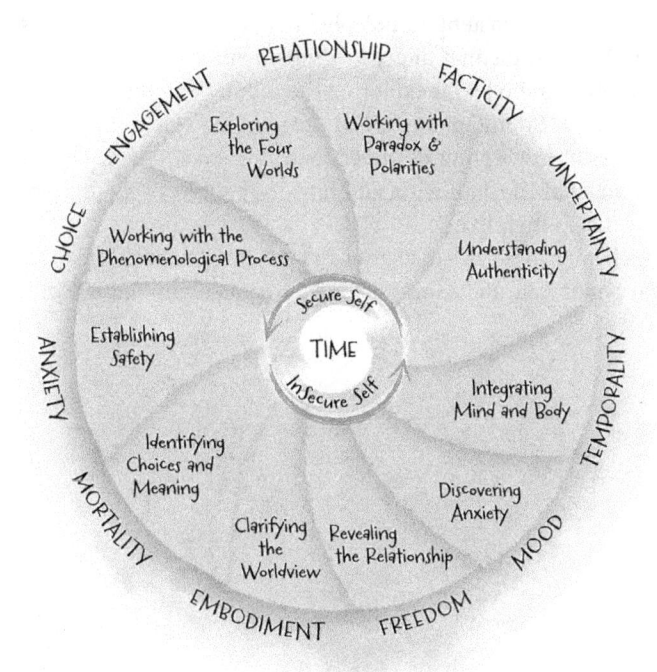

Source: Alison Strasser

Time-Limited Existential Therapy: The Wheel of Existence, Second Edition. Alison Strasser.
© 2022 John Wiley & Sons Ltd. Published 2022 by John Wiley & Sons Ltd.

Each of the sections of the Wheel of Existence is part of the process involved in existential psychotherapy as it is understood both within the therapeutic relationship and within the client's and the therapist's world.

Section II deals with the Wheel's outer layers. Chapter 5 explores in more detail the universal ontological givens and in Chapters 6 to 15 we step through the ontic 'leaves' of individual responses. The Wheel is symbolic of the existential view in that, as in the diagram of the Wheel, life may appear to us in distinct segments, yet existentialism contends that we are the sum of our parts. The person and their experience are bound inextricably together. These interconnected and overlapping sections relate directly to the practice of time-limited existential therapy, embracing the existential themes that epitomise this practice.

All layers and leaves of the Wheel of Existence are discussed in relation to time and time-limited or time-aware existential therapy.

Application to Psychotherapy

Existential therapists integrate existential and phenomenological philosophies. The two philosophies are both distinct and yet complementary. In therapy, the existential component offers a model for exploring the themes and the meanings clients bring to their world. Simultaneously, the phenomenological method of investigation is a process of attempting to understand how clients perceive and experience the phenomena of life and living and how they subjectively interpret themselves and the events in their lives.

Case vignettes (which are composites of client work) are used to bring life to the practice of existential philosophy and show how it is integrated into the Wheel in its entirety.

The Ontological Layer: Universalising

> *If emotions were universal, then in one sense he was not alone, never had been alone, and never could be alone . . . No pain or happiness was unique. All humanity drank from the same river of emotion; and by drinking, every race, religion, and nationality became one indivisible species.*
>
> Dean Koontz, *The Key to Midnight* (1979)

The outer edge of the Wheel of Existence represents what are known as the ontological concerns. I have described these as the constant 'hums of existence': they are the immutable, universal factors, the 'givens' that are common to all human beings irrespective of gender, age, or culture. These concerns are the essences of what Heidegger was attempting to describe in terms of 'being', of what already exists before we are born or 'thrown into this world'. These factors are not about our doing or acting but about the nature of 'being', the being-ness of our living or the essential structures of humanness. Rather than seeing life as composed of complete entities, forms, functions, or nouns, something we can grab hold of, existential philosophy is concerned with being-ness, 'isms', or 'verb-ings' that denote our humanness as in a continual process of moving forward.

Ontological givens are with us constantly, shifting in and out of our awareness both in terms of when we choose to place our attention on them, or when they reveal themselves to us, so that we have to pay attention to them. For instance, anxiety is one of the constant hums that I may choose to ignore, until something draws my attention towards it. I may notice a pain or ache in my solar plexus that doesn't go away, but, when I do attend to it, may realise that it's connected to an event that was hurtful, but which I had pretended was ok.

Different philosophers write about a range of different ontological givens. In this book, I have chosen the existential themes that arise, or that I notice most commonly, in my practice.

Time-Limited Existential Therapy: The Wheel of Existence, Second Edition. Alison Strasser.
© 2022 John Wiley & Sons Ltd. Published 2022 by John Wiley & Sons Ltd.

5

The Ontological 'Givens'

> *It is [our] capacity to stand outside [ourself], to know [we are] the subject as well as the object of [our] experience, to see [ourself] as the entity who is acting in the world of objects.*
>
> Rollo May, *Psychology and the Human Dilemma* (1967)

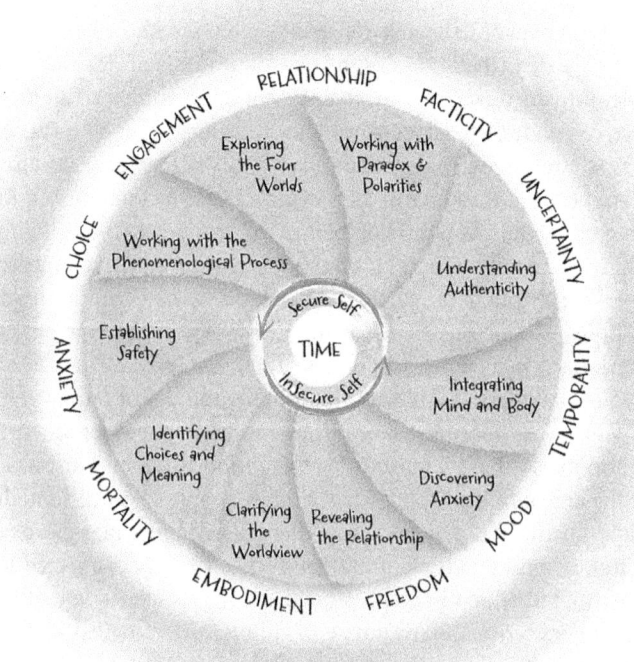

Source: Alison Strasser

Time-Limited Existential Therapy: The Wheel of Existence, Second Edition. Alison Strasser.
© 2022 John Wiley & Sons Ltd. Published 2022 by John Wiley & Sons Ltd.

Relationship

The Danish Christian philosopher Søren Kierkegaard was one of the first to emphasise the importance of subjectivity to the individual (1967). Carl Rogers (1961) elaborated on this, developing the person-centred approach to counselling where the client's subjective experience took precedence over the theory-laden, interpretative stance adopted by other therapy styles. It is the conviction that the other (the client), with the help of the therapist, can become more aware of their personal beliefs and theories, leading to more informed choices about how they function, or not, within their current ways of living.

Kierkegaard's thinking, in essence, showed that truth, by necessity, had to include this personal, subjective experience; and later, German philosopher Martin Heidegger (1962) and the French philosophers Jean-Paul Sartre (1958), Maurice Merleau-Ponty (1962), and Emmanuel Levinas (2006) added and developed this intersubjective and interrelational dimension. Intersubjectivity is the idea that our experiences, our relationships, and even our sense of identity are co-created and interconnected. There is no such thing as a human being without 'other', whether the other includes people, objects, ideas or values.

Relational understanding has become one of the foundations of existential thinking. 'Relatedness' is often described by Heidegger as 'being-in-the-world' and 'being-with-others'. In English, hyphens are used in the written form to emphasise this relational connectedness.

We are always interacting with others, from the moment we are born. This state of being is described as intersubjective, interpersonal, or interrelational and suggests that even when sitting on our own we are connected to others in our minds. The significance of interpersonal relations lies at the heart of existential philosophy

Relationship (or relatedness) in existential terms is thus a 'given' because it is not only the basis of all human interactions but is also a *sine qua non* of living.

The very essence of relationships is, however, like so much in existential thinking, paradoxical in that we are all inextricably connected to each other and yet we are separate. It is impossible to avoid being with others from our very first moments of existence. As such we are always 'with' other people, either in person or in our minds. As one of the universal ontological givens we do not exist as separate to our relationship with others and the larger environment of the world. 'Everything and everybody in the world discloses themselves by one means or another as long as they exist' (Jourard, 1971, p. 19).

Sartre (1973) describes the *interrelationship* as one where the self and other are intertwined. For Sartre, this intertwining with others is conflictual, in that each person struggles to claim their subjective identity, almost warring with the other until one party has a transitory victory. This perspective is often described as bleak in its perception of the human condition as skewed towards a state of continual conflict and its disregard of our propensity for love and intimacy. Despite this perspective, as integral to the notion of interrelatedness, Sartre (1973) also acknowledges the impact that we have on each other, that our sense of self includes the perspective of the other, a mutual being-for-others, and that there is no self without other.

Facticity

Facticity is an element of Heidegger's concept of *thrown-ness* into life, bookmarked at either end by birth and death, the timing of which we, generally, cannot control. Thrown-ness is the idea that we are thrown into the world like a die, denoting the arbitrary nature of our existence and the uncertainty of how we might land. The world we are thrown into is already in existence and we are obliged to navigate our own path. Once in the world, we always find ourselves somewhere and it is a world that we share with others.

Endings, beginnings, death, and life are all elements of our facticity, as are those aspects of being that are not created by us and are outside the realm of our human influence. These characteristics include where, what historical time, and to whom we are born, our genetic blueprint such as the colour of our eyes and our height, our family and cultural mores, and the events of our past.

Both Heidegger (1962) and Sartre (1958) refer to facticity as those characteristics of life that restrict or limit our freedom because we are not in a position to change them. In this way, facticity is bound up with the notion of limitation.

Death, of course, is the finality of our facticity. For Heidegger (1962), death is always present; it is with us from the moment we are born. In our *being-towards-death*, every moment of living is a moment of dying. However, within this facticity we have our unique, ontic experiences. We can still choose or shift our perspective to allow for new and different viewpoints to enter into our understanding. This is our personal, ontic response to the seemingly immutable feature of facticity, and will be discussed later on.

Uncertainty

Uncertainty is one of the paradoxical human tensions. From the moment of birth, we continually seek a sense of safety, a modicum of security. As babies, we seek the warmth and nurturing environment of our parents or carers. These feelings of comfort and safety remain as an implicit memory, which even as adults we constantly desire to return to. Maslow argued that after we have satisfied our basic needs, such as the need for food and shelter, we strive for protection and safety to exist in the world: 'After the bodily needs are taken care of [our needs] are for ... protection safety, security' (1968, pp. 199–200).

It is an incontrovertible fact, however, that upon first opening our eyes we are 'thrown' into a world that is inherently full of insecurity and uncertainty. As humans, we are engaged in a perennial search for certainty, safety, and to feel secure against the backdrop of a world that is replete with uncertainties and unpredictability. We struggle continuously and fight against this reality, trying to eke out some semblance of meaning, some form of security, against which we can measure ourselves as constant and safe. Paradoxically, searching for security in itself generates 'existential anxiety', which will be discussed further below.

Spinelli (2015, p. 27) describes the principle of uncertainty as that which 'expresses its presence not only in the surprising events in our lives, but just as equally and forcefully in the *expected* and (seemingly) fixed meanings and circumstances of everyday life'.

Temporality

As with both facticity and mortality (which will be explained below), the 'given' of *temporality* merges with Heidegger's concept of *thrown-ness*, the idea of being thrown into a finite life over which we have no control, as is true with both our birth and (in most cases) the timing of our death. It is our *being-towards-death* where we transcend the present and project towards the future where both our possibilities and our death are lived simultaneously. In this perspective, Heidegger understands that our facticity is the experience of living in all three (past, present, and future) dimensions of time that comes to an end with our death.

Temporality, for Heidegger, is our living in time with anticipation towards a future, the only certainty of which is known is that of death. Our past, too, is part of our present moment and bound up with our current mood and sense of possibilities.

The existentialists suggest that our acceptance of our finality can enable a more congruent way of living, with more resolute purpose and more aliveness. 'When Dasein[1] concerns itself with time, then the less time it has to lose, the more "precious" does that time become, and the handier the clock must be' (Heidegger, 1962, p. 418).

Time and temporality as one of the givens, as one of the constant hums, underpins and shapes every moment of our existence. There is no single moment when time does not exist and, as such, time is infused with what it means to be human. Time is the only ontological that is separate to our existence and will continue after our death. This is the main reason that a time-aware psychotherapy approach is a useful framework for eliciting the client's response to the constant hum of temporality.

Mood

There are many different ways of interpreting the word *mood* and we tend to fuse the terms 'mood', 'emotions', and 'feelings' as if they are identical. However, by staying with the intent of this chapter, which is to identify and explain the ontological characteristics of being human, the term 'mood' takes on a different flavour, even though our mood is revealed through our *experience* (our ontic response) of being-in-the-world.

From Heidegger's perspective, however, our moods are ontological and how we experience them is through our feelings. He contends that we are constantly attuned to the world through our mood. Mood is shaped by what is happening around us. It is also a lens through which we comprehend the world. Once again, Heidegger reveals that we are not separate entities but entangled with others, ideas, and experiences so that '[m]ood assails. It comes neither from "without" nor from "within", but rises from being-in-the-world itself as a mode of that being' (Heidegger, 1962, p. 136).

Our mood, or our particular state of mind, informs the way we see things, skews the way we interact and conversely moulds us to what is happening. Mood includes states of boredom, anxiety, anger, sadness, despair, awe or any overall disposition that influences the way we sense the world. Charles Guignon, an American philosopher and expert on Heidegger's existentialism, observes that, for Heidegger, moods 'color in advance the ways in which things can *matter* to us – whether they are amenable or irrelevant, attractive or threatening' (2009, p. 196). Hence, there is a strong connection between our mood and values.

Freedom

'Freedom is existence, and in it, existence precedes essence' (Sartre, 1958, p. 588). In this quote Sartre is stating one of the unifying principles championed by existentialists, that human beings are essentially free to choose how we act and how we respond to situations. The ontological givens, *freedom* and *choice*, are thus inextricable. This understanding of freedom implicitly denotes that we are responsible for our own meaning-making lives and cannot rely on external constructs, 'god' or a past event to indulge our desire for a sense of security.

Unsurprisingly, the concept that we are responsible for our own freedom is often hard to accept because rather than blaming others or particular situations, we are asked to understand and 'own' our part, our share of responsibility. This 'ownership' is anxiety provoking – so much so that our tendency is to avoid engaging with the authentic experience of our freedom and responsibility. Hence, Sartre adds, 'Man is condemned to be free; because once thrown into the world, he is responsible for everything he does. It is up to you to give [life] a meaning' (1958, p. 439).

For Heidegger (1962), the mood of anxiety is connected to our freedom in that anxiety pushes us into examining ourselves and our actions with the prospect of thinking freely for ourselves, and is connected to his thoughts on authenticity.

Embodiment

I exist in my body.

Jean-Paul Sartre, *Being and Nothingness* (1958)

'It is through my body that I understand other people, just as it is through my body that I perceive "things"' (Merleau-Ponty, 1962, p. 186). Similar to the concept of moods, *embodiment* as a word is an attempt to portray the significance of how our being is always integrated; our moods, our thoughts, our feelings, our senses are not individual parts to be examined separately. Indeed, we can use our ability to make sense of our bodily sensations in order to describe our feelings in a caring, thinking way. As with moods that are always there, we are permanently in the world, in our bodies – we cannot not be embodied.

Most of the existential philosophers stress our bodily existence. Kierkegaard's definition of a person is inclusive of our relations to body (1989), while Nietzsche sees the body as intrinsic to our being (1974), utilising the written form 'body-self' to depict the absence of a split. The notion of *Dasein* (Heidegger, 1962), our being, is naturally embodied in that we live and experience the world in and through our bodies.

Sartre writes evocatively about the flesh where '[t]he caress reveals the Other's flesh to myself and to the Other. . . it is my body as Flesh which causes the Other to be born' (1958, p. 459). Merleau-Ponty, a contemporary of Sartre – and also from the French school of existentialism which focused on the physical world, our body and how we exist and experience the world in an embodied manner – suggested that it is through our bodies that we come to know the world (1962).

Our embodied sense is expressed through our physical presence, our bodies and our senses. By embracing the fact that we are always in our bodies and our bodies are always in the world, an illuminating dimension supplements the more traditional verbal conversation, allowing for Merleau-Ponty's contention that 'The World and I are within one another' (1962, p. 123).

The practice of integrating the body into the therapy process will be explored in Chapter 14.

Mortality

As is the case with facticity and temporality, *mortality* relates to Heidegger's concept of *thrown-ness* into a finite life over which our control is limited. We cannot control the timing of our birth and have minimal control over the timing of our death.

Most of us, for much of our life, conceal our knowledge that death is impending by being distracted with life. Heidegger elaborates thus: '[E]vasive concealment in the face of death dominates everydayness so stubbornly that, in being with another, the "neighbours" often still keep talking the "dying person" into the belief that he will escape death and soon return to the tranquilised everydayness of the world of his concern' (1962, p. 253).

Indeed, in his book *Staring at the Sun* (2008) Yalom emphasises how our denial of our mortality is pervasive and obstructs our freedom. Heidegger (1962) makes a statement of fact that as humans we cannot but live within the incessant tension of life and living and that of death and dying. However, there is no specific rulebook on how we are supposed to live with the knowledge that we will die. It is certainly possible to live a life in evasion and some would argue that this is what 'saves' their lives.

A unique human characteristic is our ability to think of our future and to ponder our death. Existentialists believe that our ontic response will vary often according to our mood, our personal and cultural response to our idea of death and that awareness of death may give significance to living. Even within ourselves, death and dying can shift from a negative prospect to the insight that an awareness of death can provide us with zest for life and creativity. It is paradoxical that many only find this zest when death has revealed itself in its various disguises including our own or another's ill health.

Anxiety

Anxiety as an ontological given is not a state that humans may or may not acquire but is unavoidably at the centre of the human condition. It is not a peripheral threat or fear that may be classified with other reactions, but something that is rooted within our existence. Anxiety simply is anxiety and is one of the existential 'isms' (Cooper, 2003). Anxiety as an ontological given refers to a generalised sense of a life that is uncertain, unknown, and unspecific, and is connected to Heidegger's idea that we are all 'thrown' into the world (i.e. our facticity), over which we have absolutely no control and about which we have no certainty as to its meaning.

This understanding of anxiety is not related to fear or fretting but is about nothing in particular. It's an illumination of how we find ourselves and is sometimes described as one of our moods.

The ontological notion of anxiety 'seeks to convey a much more generally felt experience of incompleteness and perpetual potentiality which is expressive of an inherent openness to the unknown possibilities of life experience' (Spinelli, 2015, p. 29). The only certainty is that life in its current knowable state comes to an end, that death is universal and absolute, that we are all mortal.

How we, as humans, individually respond to this all-pervasive ontological anxiety is the specific ontic anxiety that dominates scientific and medical thinking, and will be discussed in detail in Chapter 8.

Choice

Human beings are always choosing. These actions may or may not be occurring within our awareness but are governed by another of the existential constants that are inescapable. While the limitations of our facticity are substantial, so are the possibilities from which humans can choose.

For example, we must accept the fact that we are born tall or short, that we are children of single parents, or that we come from a large family (facticity). We can do nothing about whether we are born English or Italian, for example, or the kind of culture that exists around us. Even so, we still have a choice. We have the freedom to choose the kind of attitude we will adopt towards those features and we can change our relationship to them. The existential position is united in that 'we are our choices' – that we are always choosing what we do, how we respond, and who we become. There are an infinite number of possibilities to exert one's freedom of choice.

Jaspers (1932) points out that choice is inevitably linked to anxiety. Our choices include the choice about who we are (our identity) and, simultaneously, who we are not and the choice to give up, to deny something as we face what he called 'limit situations' (*Grenzsituationen*), such as death, suffering, and the guilt that life inevitably offers. He argues that to be fully human we hold this contradictory tension, making choices both despite and because of this anxiety. In this way, freedom, choice and anxiety are inseparable. Indeed, Heidegger (1962) argues that we don't need to just collapse when we are thrown into the world. On the contrary, we are capable of understanding and are compelled to action. We can throw off our *thrown-into* condition, seize hold of our choices and their related possibilities and live life more fully. Freedom, for Heidegger (1962), is the experience of choosing to act in the world, to realise our potential, to run towards life rather than away from what is. This, he argues, is authenticity.

Engagement

Sartre specified a particular kind of authenticity when he wrote about *engagement*, defining it as a 'moral responsibility' (1973). He believed that humans are never neutral but necessarily involved in a 'project' of our own choosing. How we are committed to this project – whether fully, partially or half-heartedly – describes how we our connected to, or engaged with this venture and similarly how we act towards it.

As an ontological given, our engaging in projects not only defines us but simultaneously shapes each situation. We act on the world as the world simultaneously acts on us. For instance, one prisoner may experience his incarceration with despair and horror and his engagement might take the form of disengagement or withdrawal, while for another, the prison environment could become a place where his resolve and leadership surface.

Our 'engaging in projects' also reveals our values and what is meaningful to us. Linked to Heidegger's notion that we are all 'thrown into the world', the world of nothingness, of no intrinsic meaning, is the idea that we are necessarily impelled to choose a manner of being, a project that gives us definition, a road to walk on, and a sense of future. However, since most of these 'projects' or future ventures are chosen when we are young and lacking in greater awareness, they are usually doomed to being enacted in 'bad faith'[2] (Sartre, 1958).

Heidegger's (1962) sense of engagement relates to 'care' or '*Sorge*' which can be translated as 'concern' or 'involvement'. It is connected to his ontological sense of being-with and it reveals how we cannot but be engaged with the world that is necessarily full of other human beings.

A concluding remark. The attempt to explain ontological givens creates a textual, experiential, and philosophical conundrum. Despite the ontological dimension always existing as the background 'hum' of experience and irrespective of individual experience, this layer is impossible to describe comprehensively without including our subjective interpretation of, and the meaning we each attribute to, these givens. This very attempt at meaning-making immediately casts the discussion into the domain of ontic reactions. This conundrum confirms that the ontological layer and each of the ontic segments are in fact inextricable, and that, experientially, they occur simultaneously.

The following chapters are devoted to an application of the Wheel of Existence to the exploration of the 'ontic-ness' of individual responses within the psychotherapy setting.

Notes

1 *Dasein* is translated from the German as 'being there'; it is referring to the experience of living that is common to all human beings.
2 'Bad faith' is when, under pressure from other people and social norms, we adopt false values, thereby denying our freedom.

Stepping Through the Ontic Leaves: Individualising

I am always situated in the present on the way somewhere, as having been somewhere. Thus, experience is always in the process of becoming.
Albert Anderson, Steven Hicks and Lech Witkowski (eds),
Mythos & Logos: How to Regain the Love of Wisdom (2004)

It is difficult to define or describe concretely the essence of 'ontological', for two reasons. First, once we start to explore our living sense of our ontological experience, we become aware of how each 'given' appears tied to all the other givens, demonstrating that these cannot be viewed as separate entities but as overlapping and interconnected phenomena. Second, the ontological layer is only manifested or revealed through experience and our subjective interpretation of our experience. As soon as we attempt to put our experience into words, our experience or relationship to the givens has changed.

The segments or 'leaves' of the Wheel that circle the central core represent the dynamics of the therapeutic process and offer a way of understanding how we each individually and uniquely respond to the ontological givens. These 'leaves' are known as our 'ontic' responses and give flavour and depth to our personal being-in-the-world. The ontological given of anxiety, for example, is universal but our responses and our personal stories are unique to us.

There is always a flow, an interaction between the ontological and ontic, where the ontic is our personal and individual response and actions to 'the concrete, changing and practical aspects of existence' (van Deurzen & Adams, 2011, p. 154). The interplay, as depicted by the perforated lines, between the ontological and the various ontic segments is important in that, on the one hand, the therapist and client are sharing in the commonalities of being human while, on the other, both are responding in their distinctiveness and carving personal and particular pathways.

Time-Limited Existential Therapy: The Wheel of Existence, Second Edition. Alison Strasser.
© 2022 John Wiley & Sons Ltd. Published 2022 by John Wiley & Sons Ltd.

Indeed, the same overlapping principle of interconnectedness that was described for the ontological layer, and between the ontological and ontic layers, applies to our ontic experience. The segments are both separate and flow into each other, framing the exploration that occurs with clients. As with all themes, they can be explored individually but are not seen in isolation as everything is connected to the whole of an individual's experience.

Each of the individual segments that make up the leaves of the Wheel illustrates the principal themes that indicate our lived experience and our individual responses to the immutable, ontological givens described above. Chapters 6 to 15 will walk us through the variegated leaves of human experience and show how these may be attended to in the therapeutic encounter.

For instance, as I reflect on myself in *relationship* (an ontological given) I also experience the flutter of *anxiety* (an ontic response that includes the ontic experience, *integrating mind and body*), which arises as I get in touch with my aloneness (ontic response – *discovering anxiety*) that is a constant coming and going. Simultaneously, I notice in the same fluttering the joy and lightness of being that is part and parcel of relationship (the ontic response which is part of *clarifying worldview*) too. This anxiety is an ontological given of my 'being-in-the-world'. My experience of being in that particular relationship is my ontic reaction. The ontological structure of relatedness always includes the possibility of both the various and particular manifestations of that relationship. Thus, the universal, ontological structure of *relationship* becomes the background for the possibility of all particular (ontic) manifestations of relationship.

6

Working with the Phenomenological Process

It's no use going back to yesterday, because I was a different person then.
Lewis Carroll, *Alice's Adventures in Wonderland* (1865)

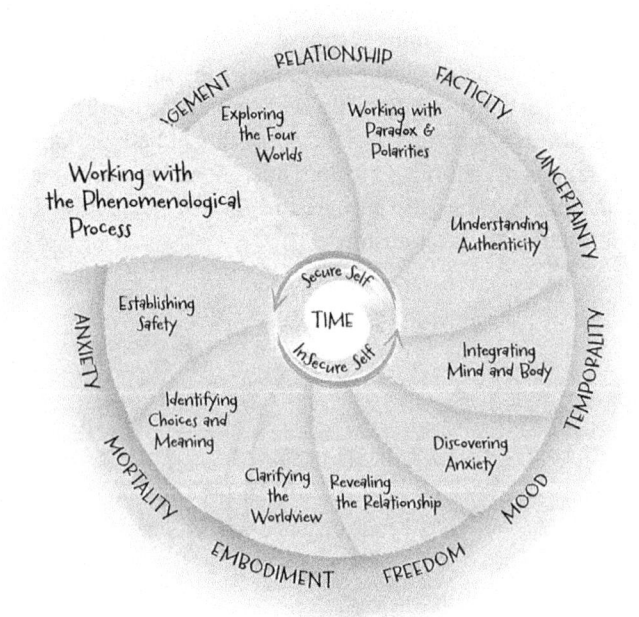

Source: Alison Strasser

Time-Limited Existential Therapy: The Wheel of Existence, Second Edition. Alison Strasser.
© 2022 John Wiley & Sons Ltd. Published 2022 by John Wiley & Sons Ltd.

As one of the segments of the Wheel of Existence, *working phenomenologically* is part of the interconnected, interwoven, and overlapping system of the ontic 'leaves'. As with all the ontic leaves, working phenomenologically connects into the ontological givens as well as into the inner segment of time and the shifting self. Working phenomenologically is the tangible practice of time-limited existential therapy, and the process of working in this way embraces the existential themes that epitomise it.

The existential therapist works both within the therapeutic relationship and with those elements of the client's and the therapist's worlds that explicitly or implicitly enter the therapy space. The therapeutic relationship and the process of therapy are themselves underpinned by the interplay of ontic responses, as depicted by the leaves of the Wheel, which come to the fore in therapy. These ontic themes signpost the significance of how our individual and unique responses to the ontological, universal givens of existence, as described in the previous chapter, are made known as we explore this phenomenological process, within the complexities and highlights of the therapeutic relationship.

As described in Chapter 1, existential therapists integrate existential and phenomenological philosophies. The two philosophies are distinct and yet complementary. In the practice of therapy, the existential component is a process of discovering what it means to be human, a basis for exploring the themes and the meanings the client brings to their world. Simultaneously, phenomenological investigation is a process of attempting to understand the question of how clients (and ourselves) *experience* phenomena or how we each subjectively interpret ourselves, the people in our life and the events that have happened. It is a way of helping us to understand and open ourselves up to all the different parts of our reality that make up our existence in our social, private, physical, and spiritual worlds.

This chapter will concentrate on the phenomenological attitude and how this translates into the time-limited therapeutic process.

Phenomenology in Brief

Stolorow writes about emotional dwelling, where 'In dwelling, essential in the pursuit of our discipline's twin goals of healing psychological wounds and exploring human nature and human existence, one leans into the other's experience and participates in it, with the aid of one's own analogous experiences' (Stolorow & Atwood, 2016, p. 103). This 'leaning into' the experience of the other elicits the telling of the unsayable by the client or that which hasn't been spoken before.

Phenomenological study can be described as the interplay of people's subjective experience of their objective world and the between-ness that inevitably emerges.

As a therapist, the process of phenomenology supports us in understanding how the client experiences their world and how they make meaning for themselves. Although often understood as solely working with people's subjective experience, phenomenology is actually about the study of phenomena as fully experienced by the person. By necessity this includes their relationship (both their experience of the other and the other's experience of them) with their external world, people, and events and thus, inevitably, the relationship with their therapist. This relationship, then, becomes integral to the therapy.

One of the aims of working phenomenologically is to support the therapist in noticing their own biases, theories, and assumptions and how these might impact on their client. Many people assume that the practice of phenomenology facilitates the therapist's neutrality. However, this is not the case. Phenomenological investigation is a vehicle to becoming more open and aware to what arises for the therapist, for the client and in the intersubjective space. In essence, the process brings out one's questioning mind within a spirit of curiosity.

Edmund Husserl (1859–1938), one of the key creators of the phenomenological approach, attempted to establish an alternative method for scientific investigations at the height of an era of reductive scientific reasoning, where objectivity was the only accepted method for scientific research. Husserl questioned the current Cartesian dichotomy between mind and body and the split between 'subject' and 'object' (Husserl, 1977). Arguing against the perspective of the time that the world was constituted from remote entities that are in some way separate from our perception of them, he developed an alternative theory that incorporated the importance of understanding the world as it is experienced in our consciousness. Through the lens of such subjective interpretation, phenomenologists can observe how people interact with themselves and with others, as well as the meaning they gain from their existence. Husserl's concern was not only with objects but with people as well – he called it *Lebenswelt*, 'the living world'.

In the process of describing phenomena there emerges an 'inseparable relationship' between human consciousness and the world. Husserl described this inevitable human characteristic as 'intentionalism', a sense of stretching towards something or someone. Human consciousness is always being directed towards the world to give meaning to it: we cannot not do so; we are thus continually making sense of our experiences, to creating awareness from our own unique, subjective position. So if I am conscious, I am always aware of something (Husserl, 1977).

Emerging from this concept of intentionality is the experiential 'proof' that the world is constantly reshaping itself in terms of the meaning we impute. There is no constant meaning, no consistent story; there is only one certainty, that of uncertainty. Change is the cornerstone of the phenomenological method whereby exploration of observable human behaviour that incorporates the inevitability of change is facilitated. In this way, phenomenological exploration becomes the primary method in an existentially oriented therapeutic approach.

The Practice of Phenomenology

Paradoxically, there are varying interpretations and differing phenomenological practices when used in both research and therapy. Spinelli (1989), following Ihde (1986), was one of the first of the existential therapists to describe a simple process of three phenomenological 'rules' that relate and define a process of phenomenological investigation with clients. These are bracketing (or epoché), phenomenological description and applying the rule of horizontalisation. While working on my doctoral thesis (Strasser, 2004), I wrote about a two-stage process of phenomenological enquiry that I now refer to as 'the phenomenological dance' which includes Spinelli's contribution. Others such as van Deurzen (2012), Adams (2013), and Langdridge (2013) have added to and complemented these steps.

The phenomenological dance has, for me, become one of the cornerstones of the practice of phenomenology, and is accompanied by two additional features: the phenomenological attitude and the spirit of relatedness. The phenomenological attitude is the way we listen to our clients' experiences, and the spirit of relatedness is about the conditions which optimise the connection between therapist and client and create the space for examining what is happening between them. The phenomenological attitude, the phenomenological dance and the spirit of relatedness are discussed below.

The practice of phenomenological enquiry is not only to open up the therapist's attitude towards the client, but also to open up the client's attitude to themselves and to the world around them.

The Phenomenological Attitude

The first assumption phenomenology describes is that all humans are biased; we view everything from our personal perspective. Our experience, our beliefs, our values, our assumptions, our special theories about life and death all influence the way that objects, people, and experiences are understood and acted upon.

A phenomenological attitude brings our attention to how much we are affected by what we hear in our client's story and how this impacts our responses. Using the idea of the 'beginner's mind', the phenomenological approach can help us to see every situation, every thought and feeling, with a new pair of eyes. 'Back to the things themselves' (Husserl, 1970) is the idea that we can attempt to understand things *as they are experienced by the client* without the imposition of our multifaceted interpretations and explanations. This attitude not only reveals our innumerable preconceptions and biases, it also gives us the opportunity to respond differently. I've used the word 'attempt' when describing the phenomenological process since it is unfeasible for humans to have absolute awareness of all things at all times. I often liken the process to the practice of mindfulness, where we 'pay attention' and begin to notice what we are doing, thinking, feeling. 'The practice of "bare attention" asks the practitioner to simply notice and to make a brief mental note of what thoughts/feelings associated with the initial noticing arise, without going into discourse or the content of it' (Nanda, 2009, p. 4).

The Phenomenological Dance

Working with the phenomenological approach or attitude can be likened to the steps or phases in a dance.

Broadly speaking, the first phase is about moving towards, stepping towards and standing close to the client, to understand their worldview. In this phase the therapist becomes attuned not only to the words the client is speaking but also to the inflections in their speech, the subtleties of their body language and even the senses arising within the body, sometimes known as the *felt-sense* (Gendlin, 1978). This attunement or 'tuning in' gives the therapist an appreciation of what is happening for the client. Broadly, this first phase includes the phenomenological processes of bracketing, description, equalisation, and attention and requires a more 'associative', resonating attitude of curiosity and *un-knowing*. These are discussed below.

In the second phase of this phenomenological dance the therapist momentarily steps away from their absorption of their client's world, while still holding the space, and begins to consider and question the client's worldview from different angles, using the information for more 'active' or challenging interventions. It's a process of the therapist imagining all possibilities and hesitantly putting these to the client, generally in the form of open questions and in a spirit of curiosity. The Wheel offers a framework for considering these various perspectives. This phase in the phenomenological dance includes the processes of horizontalisation, imaginative variation, and synthesis or verification, as discussed below.

Each interaction is different and responds to the tempo of the moment. It requires the therapist to 'become fully and thoughtfully involved. It's as if one is engaged in a dance of moving forward and moving back: one steps closer and steps away, has an effect and is affected' (Halling & Goldfarb, 1991, p. 328). It's a process of taking notice and continually taking a fresh look at situations, feelings, and thoughts. As the therapist responds to the client with this 'fresh look', so too the client starts to integrate this alternative perspective, beginning to question and challenge their own assumptions.

The following processes are distinct in intention but interwoven in practice.

First Phase of the Phenomenological Dance

Four interconnected processes (bracketing, description, equalisation, and attention), relating to the therapist's attempt to 'see' their client with fresh eyes, make up this first phase. Equally, this practice helps clients to hear, notice, and feel differently about themselves, a process underpinned by the overarching question of phenomenology: 'How can we understand anything without first understanding that which does the understanding?' (van Deurzen & Adams, 2011, p. 40). As described in Strasser and Strasser (1997), these steps usually invite an associative form of relating where both client and therapist are learning to be inclusive or are in sync with each other.

All the following practices offer ways to create the space and opportunity for the therapist to pause, notice his or her assumptions and biases, withhold these and thereby open up the space for the client to freely and safely explore and interrogate theirs. As mentioned earlier, this practice does not require that the therapist somehow becomes neutral or value free; instead it offers the opportunity for the therapist to become more attuned to their beliefs and worldview in order to suspend or bracket them and to clear the space for the client's exploration.

These techniques have certain implications. First, they obviate concerns about the constant need to formulate questions or proffer hypotheses or explanations. Second, they circumvent impulsive or ill-considered questions that reveal our immediate bias. Third, they allow for questions and interventions that are less laden with our theories and assumptions, sparing our clients our biases. Admittedly, total suspension of all our biases and assumptions is impossible, yet just the awareness of this process can make an impact on interpretation and intervention in a therapeutic situation. The important factor is to listen, understand and to check or verify with the client.

Bracketing

Existential therapists are continually attempting to understand what it means to experience the 'thing in itself' – in other words, their client and the client's particular perspectives about living and dying. To do so, we seek to suspend our theories and preconceived judgements so as to experience the situation or the client as if from their perspective. Husserl (1977) called this suspension 'bracketing', or epoché, which means placing all those biases, expectations, and prejudices temporarily into a mental bracket, a 'pause' or a holding position. It does not necessarily mean to 'throw out' but is rather a space to consider our choices.

Bracketing aligned with the spirit of curiosity gives us choice, helps the timing of interventions, and allows for silence and the possibility that interventions can be delayed. After further clarification with the client and quite often with oneself, we then compare this additional information from the client with our personal bias.

Phenomenological Description
As with bracketing, phenomenological description enables us to remain as open as possible to our client's experience without the imposition of our theories and assumptions. Phenomenological description asks the therapist to stay with the level of description rather than going to explanations or interpretations of what they believe the client might be saying. This is a qualitative, rather than quantitative, method that focuses on the way something appears and what and how it is expressed.

Staying with description offers the client the opportunity to recount an experience, rather than having to explain it, and can lead to an investigation of meaning in contrast to searching for objective facts. 'Describe, describe, describe' not only provides clients with more space to reflect and to expand on their stories and their personal theories, but, together with bracketing, also provides the therapist with the space to notice what is happening for him- or herself.

> Mark had agreed to a module of 12 sessions and at the eighth he related how his friends, yet again, had derided him for dating a girl as a way of pursuing his mother. I remember my own intake of breath and my inner groan. In bracketing my reaction, I was free to wonder, firstly, why it was necessarily wrong to be in a relationship with someone who bore similarities to one's parents and, secondly, how his friends were to know that they were correct? In other words, I was inwardly challenging my own theories and assumptions, from which bracketing freed me, to arrive at a place of openness and curiosity. My resulting question to Mark, 'what's wrong with going out with your mother?' enabled a process of phenomenological description, exploration and discovery for us both.

Equalisation
'Equalisation' suggests that any initial description of phenomena is made without priority or hierarchical importance on the part of the therapist. Equalisation is ultimately a check point to allow ourselves 'a greater degree of caution in adhering too closely or uncritically to the immediate hierarchies that we may have imposed upon our investigation from its earliest stages' (Spinelli, 2015, p. 22). By applying this notion clients can assemble and narrate their experiences in an atmosphere that is not biased or judgemental. On a practical level, this means that clients are

seen and heard for what they are, for what they are saying. Equalisation encourages us to recognise both that clients may prioritise their concerns differently to how we might do so for them and that what may be important for a client one week may have shifted in significance the next. More pertinently, the therapist does not immediately presume to know what is important in a client's initial statements.

Yet, despite our best intentions, this element of the phenomenological process is the one that we are constantly inadvertently transgressing. At each point that a therapist asks a question or makes an intervention they are making a choice about which element of what the client is saying is worthy of following through. It may be helpful, therefore, to see equalisation as an *attitude*, not a rule.

Attention

Attention, or attending to the phenomena, is a reminder for the therapist to stay with the content of what the client is describing, to 'attend only to that which appears in experience' (Langdridge, 2013). As noted before, one of the cornerstones of phenomenology is to believe the client's story, that what they are telling the therapist is their truth at a point in time. It is their narrative, their personal theory that has been created by the client him- or herself as part of their identity.

Staying with the client's current truth and entering into their worldview by the practices of bracketing, phenomenological description, equalisation, and attention offers the therapist a glimpse of what is occurring for the client and significantly opens up the space for the client to know what it is like to be believed and understood.

> When Mary recounted her history and told me, amongst other details, how her uncle had sexually abused her, it was very easy for me to conclude that Mary's adult behaviours of withdrawal, migraines, and her inability to seek friendships were directly attributable to this childhood trauma. However, Mary was insistent that her absence of 'self' and lack of direction or purpose had always been part of her personality. Abandoning my own prejudice and working with Mary's truth allowed us to explore her beliefs from a different angle. She said emphatically that she had never felt that she had a sense of self or fluidity to her life that encompassed a sense of purpose and a reason to get out of bed in the morning. By my attending to Mary's words, rather than my own hypotheses, our focus turned towards Mary's own theories and beliefs and to her desire to feel more connected to ideas, work, people, herself, and life in general.

The Mode of Associative Interventions

The four integrated processes outlined above are the moves in the first phase of the phenomenological dance (Strasser, 2004) that assist us, as therapists, to enter into and resonate with the client's world without our own prejudices and biases influencing our view. Our questions and interventions in this phase are about staying within the client's frame of reference and are described as *associative* in that the tempos of both the client and therapist are attempting to remain in sync.

Stemming from 'associative' thinking, *associative interventions* generate a contemplative, almost hypnotic state. This is the 'timeless' or 'mindless' state where the perception of 'clock time' disappears. Indeed, clients frequently comment how time becomes suspended during sessions.

During this sequence of therapy an intersubjective understanding between therapist and client will often develop and there is a natural and easy flow to the interventions. The most common interventions will consist of careful listening and 'being' with the client, enabling the therapist to reflect back moods, feelings, and content, to summarise, to note any body language signs, monosyllabic prompting, and, most important of all, to remain silent. 'Meaning by dialogue', according to Martin Buber, is 'not just talking. Dialogue can be silence' (1990, p. 53). Sometimes called 'presence', it is when two (and sometimes more) people are fully present with each other. Carl Rogers described it thus:

> I find that when I am the closest to my inner, intuitive self – when perhaps I am somehow in touch with the unknown in me – when perhaps I am in a slightly altered state of consciousness in the relationship, then whatever I do seems to be full of healing. Then simply my presence is releasing and helpful. At those moments, it seems that my inner spirit has reached out and touched the inner spirit of the other. Our relationship transcends itself, and has become part of something larger. Profound growth and healing are present. (Baldwin, 2000, p. 36)

These 'timeless' mergings of the thoughts and feelings between therapist and client are often when insights occur. For Martin Buber, these are the Thou and I empathic moments that are the result of 'human effective dialogue' (Buber, 1990, p. 53). In these I/Thou moments, it is more than the merging of two people. As each person comes together they retain their personal sense of I whilst resonating and accepting the other.

Second Phase of the Phenomenological Dance

This stage of the dance (Strasser, 2004; Strasser & Strasser, 1997) is more active or challenging in nature and asks the client to reflect in a different, more dynamic way about their understanding of their world, through the processes of horizontalisation, imaginative variation and synthesis and verification. Interventions by the therapist might also include questions or reflections that may challenge the client's current perceptions and highlight discrepancies or contradictions, as well as suggesting alternative ways of viewing their understanding. It will also include drawing on existential philosophy as a basis for listening and asking questions. Although described as distinct, in practice they form part of the whole process of 'tuning out' to reap new perspectives, exploring other segments of the client's story. Yet in this 'tuning out' we still embrace the client's story and resonate with their truth.

Horizontalisation
In contrast to the first stage where the therapist enters and explores the client's world 'as if' they were the client, horizontalisation is about exploring the client's story within their larger context. Quite literally, this is about placing the client's worldview within the 'horizons' of their world. Martin Adams describes this as 'the bridge', 'when what is becoming known is placed against a horizon, in a context, and simply placing the experience in a context can give it a broader meaning' (2013, p. 60).

> Returning to Mary, her lifelong search was to find a purpose, a reason to get out of bed in the morning. We spent many sessions getting 'lost' in her world, a state of being which was consistent with us being in the first phase of the phenomenological dance and a reflection of how she spent most of her days and nights, except when she was forced into work to earn money. As I gained more knowledge of Mary's background and values, I was able to both hold her everyday living experience and to stand aside, asking questions that took into account the broader picture. It became obvious that connected to Mary's overall sense of self and purpose was her need to be creative. Taking this picture of creativity, we placed it within the context of Mary's world (horizontalisation). She was born as the middle child of a family of six in a small country town. Using my knowledge of Australian country towns and questioning what it must have been like for a bright, inquisitive child like Mary, we were able to understand that she was bored, uninspired, and had always felt on the outside of her family and community. Through this process, we understood that her desire to be creative was a path out of her run-of-the-mill existence. It was her escape and her reason for living.

Imaginative Variation
Imaginative variation involves the phenomenological process of shifting sideways: the therapist steps aside from the immediacy and imagines alternative scenarios for the client that inform the questions.

Working with imaginative variation in conjunction with the Wheel of Existence is where the interplay of the entire Wheel comes to the fore. By focusing on what the client is saying or how they are presenting, one can imaginatively reflect on each section of the Wheel to find questions or interventions to expand the client's experience.

The step of imaginative variation assists the therapist in locating and pulling together the repeating patterns that occur in a client's life – or more accurately, their perception of the events in their life and the meaning they have imbued them with. It brings to the fore the process of reflecting and asking about alternative perceptions, thoughts or other scenarios which might open up the client's world to new insights.

> Mary and I spent many hours exploring her I-sense of her world, her lack of meaning and purpose and her desire and ability to disappear into fantasy lives of others in novels and films. She described her love of dance parties and the accompanying sense of anonymity and abandonment of her body as she literally danced into the depths of the night. Although I might not feel similarly when dancing, my sense of exhilaration from snow skiing helped me identify with Mary's feeling and attune to her. Using my attuned connection with her, I could also imagine other scenarios which affected her.

Synthesis and Verification

Synthesis and verification in this second phase of the phenomenological dance have two functions: extending the content of the client's narrative and broadening their personal sense of meaning and understanding of who they are. As with all these phenomenological processes, all steps are interconnected; they can happen in any order and one intervention may cover more than one function.

The therapist continually checks back with the client to ensure that what they have heard is correct. Verification is the step in the dance that ensures that the client is understood. Synthesis occurs when the therapist brings the various threads of the story into a succinct whole, and is often met with the client's wholehearted agreement and a sense of relief. Often the client will slightly change or add to this synthesis, which in itself brings greater clarity and validation to their story.

The therapist might speculate about links or patterns they've noticed in the client's world; they might point out discrepancies or contractions in the narrative or indeed explore meanings that are not transparent. 'It is about wondering about how all the elements are related. We are wondering what similarities there are, and how the jigsaw fits together, for fit together it must' (van Deurzen & Adams, 2011, p. 51).

> Piecing together, or synthesising, the threads of Mary's story led to my observation that her pattern of not feeling seen or heard was significant in her childhood stories both within the family and in school, and, as a theme, still retained its poignancy in her current world. Mary responded in agreement.

To do this step justice, the therapist stays empathically attuned to what the client is saying.

The Mode of Stepping Back and Tuning Out: Challenging and Active Intervention

Horizontalisation, imaginative variation and synthesis and verification are the three actions in the phenomenological process that embrace the therapist *stepping back* from the total absorption into the client's world, a sort of *tuning out* by the therapist to consider and reflect on contradictions that might have arisen or to bring into the conversation other information and insights that might inform the client's world. While the focus still lies with the client, on their theories and assumptions of how they have come to be the person they have become, the therapist's questioning and interventions are now more active or challenging. This can include the therapist speaking about their experience of what is occurring in the therapeutic space, so that its impact on, and meaning for the client can be reflected upon and understood in the same way that any other ontic experience would.

Active interventions challenge the client's perceptions and pick up on any discrepancies that might have emerged. The very nature of 'challenging' and the notion of active intervention will by definition interrupt the client's associative and narrative mood. It will provoke them to transcend into a different plane – that of thinking – and will evoke an active and didactic thinking process. Yet this mode of enquiry still attends to the client's sense of their world, adding other dimensions or alternative perspectives which the client can choose, or not, to take on board. Since this is a phenomenological enquiry, the interventions emerge from what the client has implied or stated rather than from an external theoretical or psychological theory of the personality.

Discrepancies highlight the polarities of existence, the idea that there are two ways in which to view every experience. Thus, what may appear to be a positive experience will also have its negative components.

> Marjorie believed that success came through earning money, yet at the same time she believed that money was the root of all evil. Money for Marjorie was positive because the more she earned, the more her goals were realised. The negative side, however, was that she got little pleasure in the possession of

> money per se. She preferred to live like a pauper 'because money was the root of all evil'.
> My challenge was to point out to Marjorie these two positions and to enquire, in a spirit of empathic curiosity, as to how she lived with both of them. Often when these contradictions are mentioned, the response is one of shock or amazement. Marjorie shook her head, laughed, and then sank into a quiet but questioning place. We then spent many hours unpicking and exploring her relationship to success and failure. Eventually, Marjorie became more flexible around these definitions which translated into actions that were less punishing and more rewarding.

Challenging, like the associative interventions, must follow the client's train of thought. There should be no hidden agenda in the way a therapist intervenes, for challenging is asking the client to elucidate and to reflect on or sense more deeply the material they bring up themselves. Sometimes called 'experiencing near', it is almost as if the challenge is something the client already knows. It is through challenging the client that discrepancies are brought into awareness and sharper focus, where words, images or symbols emerge to bring a new meaning to the whole.

The Flow of the Dance

Each of these phases of the phenomenological dance are equally valuable in that they enable the therapist to feel attuned to the client's world. Attunement countenances the shift into a more challenging position which can include either a probing, yet curious intervention or a reflective but questioning attitude in which particular patterns or responses from the client might be noticed by the therapist. Such noticing may lead, in turn, to an exploration of their gaps or blind spots.

The two phases of the dance each have their own tempo depending on the rhythm of the interplay between client and therapist. Sometimes the dance is slow and intimate, and the attention remains more firmly in the associative position. Insights are more immediate or reflexive, emerging in the space in between. The second phase, which is also reflective, may be more considered or thoughtful. This is also where occurrences in the therapeutic relationship are discussed, not just experienced. The dance can easily shift from slow to a quicker tempo where the therapist and client flow from an associative or 'tuning in' stance to the challenging or 'tuning out' stance at quite a pace.

> I search for connection and emotional resonance with the person I am with, trying to locate their vulnerability and the pulse of their life. My observations tend to begin after I have calmed myself enough to focus on

the other rather than on myself. I seek to sense their central concern and try to understand their position and way of being present in their world before I began to speak. My understanding comes from my senses first and then gets refined by my feelings and reactions, and them it is adjusted and corrected by my reflection, and by our exchanges of words and the mental images I am forming and articulating. (van Deurzen & Baker, 2019, p. 182)

The Spirit of Relatedness

The phenomenological approach with its phases and methods helps both the therapist and client become aware of the smorgasbord of beliefs, values, assumptions and feelings that influence the way we live. It is a process that we learn and also one that emerges within the intersubjective space as the flow of the dance is created.

The therapeutic encounter is seen as microcosm of the client's world of relationships and so how both the therapist and client meet each other is part of the curious enquiry that takes place. At its core is the desire to generate a relatedness between therapist and client that brings forth a depth of connection and a space for an understanding of what is occurring between both people. Sometimes known as intersubjectivity, this connection is about discovering truth and meaning in the place of togetherness. Stolorow (Stolorow & Atwood, 2016, p. 103) talks about 'emotional dwelling' as a process of 'leaning into' and 'participating' in the other's experience and to speak the unsayable with gravity and truth.

The Art of the Question

Questions are as much an invitation for the client to know more about themselves as for the therapist to learn about the client. Here, a spirit of curiosity and the presence of un-knowing are critical. Generally, questions fall into two categories: those that are asking about the story, the 'what' of the client's experience, which Husserl (1970) calls *noema*, and those questions that consider the 'how' of the client's experience, which he calls *noesis*. These 'how' or noetic questions refer to the client's perception of their experience inclusive of their bodily senses and feelings. Noema and noesis are side-by-side correlates stemming from Husserl's concept of intentionality to show that awareness is always directed somewhere, whether real or imagined.

The way we ask the question, the tone and the pacing of our voice, is by necessity going to influence the answer we get. Additionally our 'pre-understanding' (Heidegger, 1962) will influence what we hear since our only means of interpreting is from our own understanding of the world.

The Expression of Descriptive Interpretation

A moot point amongst therapists is what constitutes an interpretation? As noted above, the phenomenological position states clearly the necessity for description rather than interpretation or explanation. It is only possible to interpret if there is a theory to interpret from. Psychoanalysts, for instance, will interpret resistance, transference and dreams from a theory-driven perspective in order to aid the process of bringing unconscious material into consciousness. While the response of the client and the client's history and personality are taken into account, interpreting goes 'beyond what is readily observable and [allows us to] assign meaning and causality to a psychological phenomenon' (Greenson, 1967, p. 39).

Chambers 21st Century Dictionary defines the word 'interpret' as 'to explain the meaning of . . . to consider or understand'(2021). In existential therapy, the therapist is the facilitator of interpretation as opposed to the interpreter. After a combination of challenging and associative-type questions, the therapist might conceive a notion about the client and through synthesis and verification may link certain themes together and then ask more specific questions, until the client can make his or her own connection and interpretation. The 'interpretation' that is formed by the therapist is based on a resonance with the client and a series of 'wonderings' or musings together about aspects of the client's world.

> Rebecca would say that she went blank when certain types of questions which related to her feelings were asked. She also had the habit of laughing and making jokes at these junctures. Although I could empathise with her laughter, I also wondered about what instigated this response whenever we talked about more painful areas of her life. When this observation was pointed out to her, her reaction was to laugh. At our next session Rebecca said that she felt as if she had been hit in the stomach and now realised that her natural reaction was to laugh rather than to reveal to herself and to others the inconceivable pain she felt. Rebecca had made her own interpretation.

The Attitude of Un-knowing

In reality, the therapist only has an inkling of what the client is experiencing. Karl Jaspers (1963) used the term 'not-knowing' and Spinelli (2007) expresses it as 'un-knowing' to convey not just an attitude but a truth. In adopting a phenomenological stance, this position of un-knowing asks us, first, to question even what we think we know so that we can ask, look, re-examine all aspects of what the client is describing. Second, and less obviously, to probe or to question what one 'knows', so that this knowledge is consciously 'dropped', opens up the space for both the client and therapist to question, reflect upon, and broaden their understanding. Third, it is in this un-knowing space that something un-knowable will arise.

> In supervision, Leonie talked about the loss her client felt as her last child left home to go to university. On asking Leonie to describe the loss in more detail, she paused and realised that she had assumed a knowledge about loss that was underpinned either by her (Leonie's) personal story or by the numerous theories about loss. Either way, she had forgotten to ask the client about the loss. In the subsequent supervision session Leonie had much more to say. Once prompted, her client had spent the session talking not only about her initial story but also about earlier losses and the impact on her sense of identity as a mother, wife, and woman in society. The ability of the therapist to notice what is 'known' and solicit the attitude of un-knowing is a wondrous and often scary position to take, due to the uncertainty of what may arise. To take this step also helps to avoid personal judgements that naturally arise between two people. The state of un-knowing or staying curious sanctions a more open attitude, often reversing our initial perceptions.

I'm sensitive to the idea that if I become too certain about my work with a client, it is often a warning sign that I am 'leaping in', not staying with my anxiety generated by un-knowing and not allowing the client their freedom and space to explore and find their own answers. Paradoxically, to sit with un-knowing requires us to be comfortable with the possibility of surprise. The reality is that we do not really know what is happening with our clients either in the session or in their external world.

Conversing with a Dialogical Stance

Often written about and often underestimated is the power of the conversation or dialogue between two people who can hear each other without making assumptions, 'leaping ahead' (Heidegger, 1962) or 'leaping in' (ibid.), responding on behalf of the client, in a more advice-giving approach. Allowing clients to hear their own words, assume their own responsibility, find their own answers, and be heard in their conversing is fundamental to therapy. Dialogue rather than monologue is where the therapist becomes integral to a story, by facilitating an 'open dialogue [which] is more than just a conversation; it is a joint search for personal meaning while keeping the wider picture of life in mind' (Adams, 2013, p. 41).

The Conundrum of Technique

Although written as a series of steps, there's a danger of wishing to conquer the 'method' by adopting it as a skill or as a technique that can be learnt. Instead, these 'steps' enable a richer and more respectful experience of our client's world. The moment we consider this phenomenological method of exploration to be a technique, we have negated the intention of process and the intended spirit of enquiry. Although phenomenology was not intended as a mode of therapeutic practice when described by Husserl, many of the 'helping' professions have adopted and adapted the concepts to suit their specific requirements. Technique and theory can impede the natural flow of the relationship between client and therapist. In phenomenological terms, therefore, we must attempt to 'bracket' or put aside both the structure and the Wheel when working with a client and attempt above all to remain 'human'.

In existential psychotherapy, the key components discussed in this chapter – the art of questioning and interpretation, the attitude of un-knowing and the inclusivity of the dialogic stance – have evolved in keeping with phenomenology-in-practice and maintain a spirit of relatedness. Yet, it is our very 'humanness' that lies at the heart of the phenomenological process and that informs the way we create a space safe enough for our clients to wend their ways through the challenges and offerings of their psychotherapy journeys.

7

Establishing Safety

Our anxiety does not come from thinking about the future, but from wanting to control it.

Kahil Gibran, *The prophet* (1923)

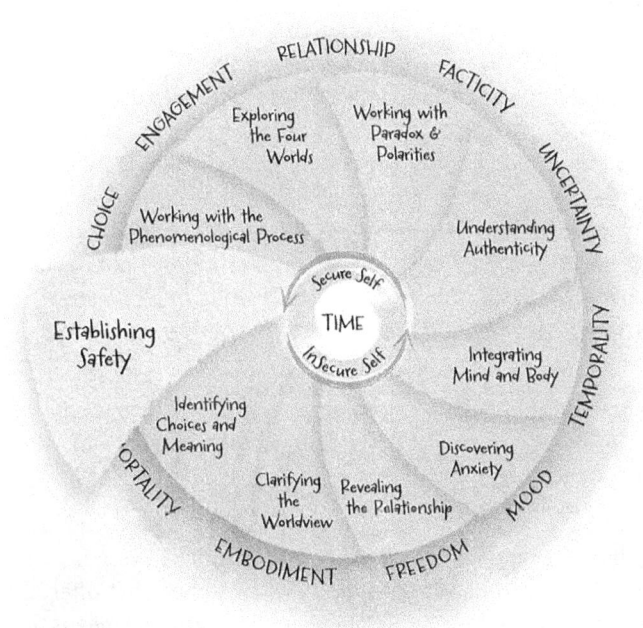

Source: Alison Strasser

Uncertainty was described in Chapter 1 as one of the ontological givens and, as such, it underpins and weaves its way through all the ontic leaves, manifesting often as an uncomfortable, and even unbearable, state of anxiety.

In the process of trying to alleviate the anxiety that uncertainty generates, to create certainty and to protect the little security that we do find, we develop an infinite number of coping strategies. We may be drawn to devising elaborate rituals and routines and creating magical thoughts to counter the often unsettling fact of our anxiety. The search for security can take many forms, such as an expectation that we may place on our relationships, a longing for religion or a passion for work. The notion of safety and the infinite number of strategies people have created to maintain a semblance of certainty is extremely important to explore with our clients.

> From a very early age, Gary believed that he could go through life without encountering obstacles or anxieties. He needed only to stay within the parameters of his parental values – to be a good enough son by being an obedient boy, a conscientious student and a good athlete. By achieving these goals, he could become a happy person. To a certain extent he had succeeded in this by conforming, by not taking risks, by withdrawing from relationships and generally by removing himself from all social contact. These were all strategies to avoid connecting with his inner torment. When his first major crisis occurred, Gary collapsed completely. He did not want to experience, nor could he cope with, any negative feelings or even a hint of anxiety. He believed that 'life needs to be smooth and anxiety-free and in my judgement', he offered, 'my norm is conformity. I could only exist in a positive way if I lived without obstacles and anxiety. When my relationship didn't work out, and I finally met with failure, the repercussions were huge!'

Although uncertainty and the seeking of certainty is an ontological given, the manner in which we each seek this safety is unique to each person – in other words, an individual ontic response.

> In contrast to Gary, James enjoyed the thrill of riding motorbikes very fast. It was the excitement of the speed and the feeling of being alive that offered him, perhaps somewhat paradoxically, his safety, his security, and the means to his sense of certainty that he was alive and kicking. Without this thrill, or the anticipation of this thrill, James described himself as dead. However, James's behaviour caused his wife to feel anxious; she didn't appreciate James's passion, failing to understand how his riding was intrinsic to his relationship with life. Banned by her from riding, he sank into great depths of despair, using marijuana to self-medicate.

Contracting in Therapy

The therapy frame mirrors the paradox of our ontic response to anxiety, where the contracting and the setting up of boundaries create an artifice of safety. As discussed in Chapter 3, setting firm boundaries as part of the initial contracting helps to set up the consistency and predictability that clients can rely on. Although to some extent the creation of this kind of consistent environment is an artificial situation, it can be helpful in raising for exploration the illusory nature of clients' notions of safety.

As with other modalities, the frame is the contractual agreement with the client and includes negotiation about time, fees, cancellation policies, confidentiality, contact outside of sessions, breaks from therapy and attention to the physical setting. Clients' responses to such boundaries reveal their own interesting stratagems.

> Doris was always 2 minutes late for her sessions. Even if she were early, I would hear her pacing outside my gate, only to arrive 2 minutes after the scheduled start of her sessions. Although it was not immediately obvious from her nonchalant manner, Doris was shy and lacking in self-esteem and it emerged through our exploration that her late arrival would give her a sense of safety, ensuring she wouldn't bump into any clients who were leaving. In her everyday life, Doris similarly arrived at social events late so that she could merge into the crowd and choose whom she was going to speak to.

> Neville could never hand over his payment in person and would push the cash under my front door within half an hour of completing his session. Our exploration into this pattern revealed that he didn't want to confront the fact that he had to pay someone for contact and intimacy. To Neville, it felt similar to paying to have sex with a prostitute.

Boundaries are about providing a safe and secure environment for clients to disclose and express themselves freely. Often misunderstood as rules, the frame is, in fact, the container or the backbone from which the client can reveal their idiosyncratic predispositions.

> Janice would periodically storm out of our sessions and return the next week full of apologies. The knowledge that she had a fixed date for her therapy sessions in her diary gave her permission to reveal her anger. Eventually, Janice

> apologised, revealing that in her dislike of confrontation, she would manipulate the situation so that she could feel rejected. This would neatly corroborate her belief that she was dislikeable.

Sometimes forgotten, but of equal significance, is that the frame includes the setting and layout of the consultancy room.

> My therapy room revealed Mark and Jenny's differences when describing their ideal home. Mark loved sitting on the sofa looking out at the garden, while Jenny only felt secure huddled in the armchair that had its back to the outside world. In life, Mark wished to live in the country and Jenny wanted to live in a contained unit in the heart of a city, preferably on the top floor. Their individual feelings of physical space became one of our metaphors when exploring their differences in expectations for both their relationship and life in general.

Within the time-limited awareness frame, the contracting period is also the place to reflect on clients' very personal (ontic) responses to the ending.

> When discussing his expectations around ending, Robert did not want to restrict himself to a time-specific structure and we contracted to keep reviewing, to see how this desire for an unspecified end might connect to some of the issues he wished to explore. His father died when he was 12 and, during our time together, we found that he had a group of very loyal and close male friendships that felt eternal. Yet his experience of relating with women seesawed between them being too close for comfort or too distant and impersonal. In the latter situation, with women, he found reasons to leave, remaining firmly in control of the ending. Similarly, he wanted to assess for himself when and how he wished to finish our time in therapy.

We tend to think of endings as absolute rather than a point in the 'time' continuum. Often, clients perceive the end of therapy as a type of abandonment, as final, with nothing beyond that shutting of the therapeutic door, a kind of 'death'. However, there are beginnings in endings and new possibilities that cannot yet be envisioned. The modular frame offers the potential for a second series of sessions, usually after a gap of a couple of months. Similarly, clients in open-ended therapy will finish and may return, often many years later. There's a sense that an end of one episode and the start of a new episode can precipitate something new. If clients return after a period of time, it is like a new chapter, a new beginning, a series with episodes that continues to unfold. Circumstances such as holidays or any breaks from therapy are also forms of endings and these types of interruptions also alert us to the necessity of understanding that the world we live in is ever-changing and finite.

It is often the accidental deviations from the boundaries that can facilitate a dramatic change, as long as talking about the issues involved can be incorporated into the therapy.

> During the eighth of 12 sessions with Paul, I (believing it to be the tenth session) asked how Paul felt about having only two sessions left. Paul was visibly distraught and expressed profound bafflement, saying, 'This is only our eighth session and I'm sure we have another four left before we finish.' After further discussion, Paul revealed that at that moment he had lost complete confidence in me. He felt that there was no concern or care about his own wellbeing. Indeed, had I known the correct ending date, he would have felt confident that I would continue to care for him even after the conclusion of therapy. During the following sessions and following a conversation between us about this difficult disruption, Paul eventually came to the conclusion that I, too, was only human and capable of making mistakes. He realised that the therapeutic environment was also subject to the same kind of uncertainties that he experienced in everyday life.

It is equally important to explore clients' feelings and attitudes towards endings in the case of brief therapy where there may seem no apparent opportunity for further sessions, where the finality is fixed. Furthermore, in brief therapy, the emotional impact of ending may precipitate clients getting in touch with their feelings about ending quicker than with ongoing therapy.

> In the eleventh of 12 sessions, Dora arrived late and was monosyllabic. She kept looking to me to initiate our conversation. Thirty-five minutes into our session, she burst into tears, saying how sad she felt and that now, most of all, she had let me down by not being adult about leaving. Dora's belief that she had to be grown up arose when her parents separated and at the age of 8 she took on the responsibility of looking after her mother. As we talked about our imminent ending, her belief that she should bottle her emotions and shouldn't show her sadness emerged. We parted with my acknowledging her sadness and how it was natural to feel that way. I too expressed my sadness at our parting. In our final session, Dora revealed her ambivalence about

> having to be 'grown up', how she had remained in a child role in her current relationship and what it would mean for both her and her partner if she became more responsible. We parted with Dora expressing her intention to introduce new behaviours and to initiate, rather than react to, conversations with her partner.

Themes that portray how clients negotiate their own endings may emerge in their initial story.

> Martin was very clear in our first session that he had an array of strategies to not feel rejected, including leaving friendships, work, and girlfriends before he was rebuffed. This approach to ending became a contracting point in that we agreed that I would raise the option of ending the therapy if I felt Martin's reluctance to continue and I asked him to do the same. Seven months later, he began to cancel sessions with the excuse that work was demanding his attention. On further prompting, Martin revealed that he was embarrassed and ashamed because he had returned to a previously abusive relationship and did not want me to think ill of him, which he was concerned would lead to my ultimate rejection of him.

> Conversely, Marina arrived confidently, stating that 'I had her for life'. Although uttered in jest, our exploration of her statement revealed that her humour disguised her sheer fear of loneliness. One of her tactics was to have people on whom she could rely strategically placed around her in order to counter these feelings. Paradoxically, although Marina had fantasies of an intimate relationship, she was scared of being suffocated and having to live someone else's life. She preferred to live on her own but was terrified of her aloneness. This became the major theme of our work.

Time is not only implicit in all our work but will reveal itself in many guises to be worked with and understood by both client and therapist.

> Maureen was returning to her home in the USA in 8 weeks, so the boundary and her motivation to work within the time frame were clear. She had been dismissed from her workplace and, since she was on a specific work visa, her only option was to return home. Over the four years she had worked and lived in Sydney she had, for the first time in many years, begun to put her roots down and to feel at home. She had been planning and working with her team

who were excited about the future. Hence, at first glance, Maureen's dismissal seemed out of the blue and cruel. Maureen was in shock and found herself unable to stop sobbing. This crying intensified when she went to work and heard her boss's voice. Over the ensuing 8 weeks Maureen was able to shift from this initial shock to a wider perspective on the situation, including how she 'knew' but ignored the signs that her visa was not going to be renewed. She was an enchanting person and worked well with bosses that were known to be difficult, so at the back of her mind she imagined she could win this current boss over. The revelation that her usual charm had not worked was a jolt and an impetus to be more on the alert and less reliant on her ability to charm. Although our ending was sad, mirroring the many goodbyes she had to say, she left with a renewed sense of other beginnings, including the option of returning to Sydney at a later time.

Edna exemplified how time and her fear of separation were of paramount significance in her therapy. Everything appeared to be proceeding smoothly, but as we reached the second half (around the sixth session) Edna was shocked to realise that although she could remember and talk about her childhood experiences and traumas, she was unable to recollect any feelings. It was just a story that she had narrated, devoid of emotion. Not only was she not able to understand why this was happening, she also felt totally incompetent.

In the same way that Edna could not express or feel her pain, she was also seemingly unaffected by the impending termination of therapy. Without warning, at the eighth session, Edna began accusing me of abandoning her and treating her in the same abusive way as her parents and her boyfriends had treated her. After her tirade of anger, she began to sob uncontrollably.

Paradoxically, at this moment Edna was experiencing her feelings and, as we gently probed, she suddenly shrieked that she was remembering her feelings of rejection and desertion when she had found her mother in bed with a strange man. Edna's feelings now tumbled out and, over subsequent sessions, she talked about her parents, boyfriends, husbands and friends in a different way. She realised that her fear of rejection had impeded many aspects of her life including her desire to write. In the eleventh session, she brought a beautifully crafted essay about her therapy, and she continued to explore her wish and intention to write.

In this case, the time limit of 12 sessions acted as a pressure valve that eventually exploded in the form of extreme anger at the impending abandonment by her therapist. It was as if the anger served as a release allowing Edna to get in touch with her feelings. It is extremely rare for a client not to have some kind of reaction to the impending termination, whether the sessions are brief, modular or open-ended.

The Constancy of Time

It is not only endings that are spoken about when working within a time-aware approach. The perception and awareness of how the time-related elements of the therapy process are experienced – in other words, the ontic response – will shift for both therapist and client and are facets for exploration by the therapist both with the client and in supervision.

Time is also a consideration when reflecting on the actual timing of interventions and will vary according to the bounds of time. Within a session, I may decide not to follow through with a thought if the end is close. Clients, though, often use their last few minutes to reveal a delicate confidence.

> Each week, Martha had several issues she wanted to talk about. I noticed how she would start with the least important, showing her impatience by looking at her watch with a painstaking frown if I stopped her flow at a point that she did not consider central to her story. She knew her sessions were 50 minutes and she wanted to be in control of her time. By actively working with my observation in her therapy, Martha's desire to manage the sessions lessened over the three years of her therapy, during which time we worked through how she was not only managing herself but also me.

> Tim would inevitably get overwhelmed and emotional about 5 minutes before the end of each session. He would attempt to stand up and then sit down again, asking for time to gather his senses. His request for more time became a symbol of our work together and mirrored his struggle with the unexpected deaths he had faced, starting with the premature death of his daughter at 3 months.

We can and do feel periods of certainty and safety but they never last, and in many ways, providing a safe environment for clients is also a paradoxical exercise. While therapy strives to provide safety, it also aims to allow clients to become aware that the world inside and outside the therapy walls is a world of uncertainty. Therapy can support clients to recognise the fallible strategies they have constructed to provide the illusion of certainty and provide guidance in finding their own voice within uncertainty, insecurity, and anxiety. Paradoxically, it is within these realms that we may be presented with opportunities to face, and engage with, the anxiety which underpins or permeates our lives, and thereby to change and grow.

8

Discovering Anxiety

All of your anxiety is because of your desire for harmony. Seek disharmony and you will gain peace.

Rumi, *The Love Poems of Rumi* (1993)

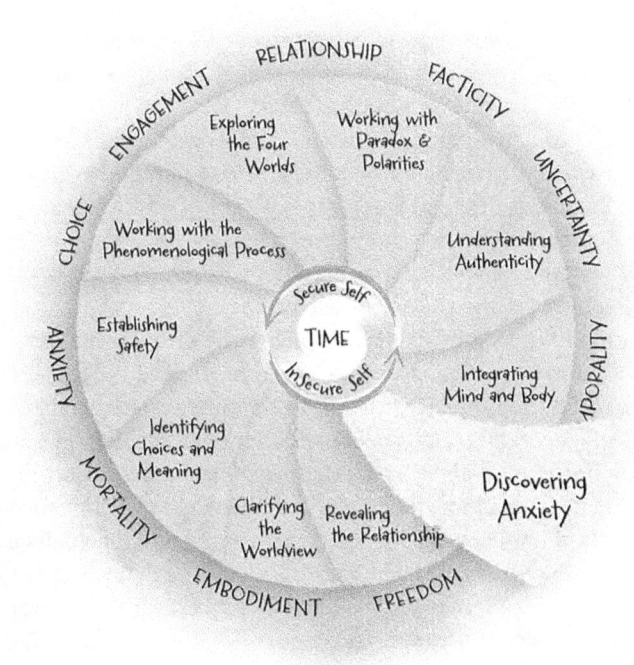

Source: Alison Strasser

Time-Limited Existential Therapy: The Wheel of Existence, Second Edition. Alison Strasser.
© 2022 John Wiley & Sons Ltd. Published 2022 by John Wiley & Sons Ltd.

As discussed in Chapter 5, anxiety is one of the ontological givens of existence. The hum of anxiety is a constant background whine, and without it we would probably not have any sense of feeling alive, in all of our fluctuating states of happiness and despair. Yet as we know so well, anxiety is also a personal way of responding to the vagaries and uncertainties of life and reveals how we are attuned (or not) to the existential givens. Our responses to the ontological hum of anxiety, our ontic response, reflects our relationship to anxiety and includes our responses, how we experience our anxiety and how we make meaning of this experience.

An overarching theme that unites all existential philosophers and practitioners is that both anxiety and its symptoms are not to be avoided but are something to be faced. Anxiety is viewed as an alarm clock, the wake-up call and a constant reminder that we are alive. We can choose to avoid, evade, and mask our anxiety or we can see it as the instigator of discovery and change.

As we all know too well, anxiety may be *felt* as fear. This is one of the many ontic responses we have to that ontological anxiety as described in Chapter 5. A feeling of fear or feelings of anxiety trigger, in a primitive part of the brain, a range of protective fight, flight or freeze responses that are designed to keep us safe from potential dangers. There are also the many forms of fears or anxieties that connect to our life's experiences and which relate to our personal principles and sedimented beliefs, as will be elucidated upon in Chapter 10.

We can feel a range of anxious responses, from a mild noticing of feeling uncomfortable to overt and particularly visible forms of fear. These may be labelled as depression, stress or phobias, for example, but our experiences of anxiety are all 'natural human responses to the commonplace tragedies of everyday life' (Adams, 2013, p. 102), and by exploring them through an existential lens we discover how they are connected to the givens of existence.

People talk about *existential anxiety* as a feeling of anguish or dread that is not only experienced as a threat to being, but is also 'the experience of the threat of imminent non-being' (May, 1983, p. 109). We may become anxious when we become aware of who we fundamentally are, of our actions and the strategies we employ to deny or evade our essential selves. Existential anxiety is the anxiety that emanates from running away, from imagining – or even pretending to ourselves – that life, or any elements of our lived experience, is different to how it actually is. This is the anxiety of *inauthenticity* (Heidegger, 1962) and living in *bad faith* (Sartre, 1958). Yalom (1980) highlighted four defences or concerns that arise from existential anxiety: those of death, freedom, existential isolation, and meaninglessness, while Spinelli's concept of 'worlding' (2007, 2015) incorporates the ontological given of uncertainty as a place of un-knowing, of chaos, ambiguity, meaningless, and the absence of structure, where we cannot grasp reality. 'Worlding' refers to a state that is pre-reflective, non-verbal, and is underpinned by existential anxiety.

As humans we are continually navigating the existential givens and making choices, whether we like it or not, and whether we're aware of doing so or not. We are continually shifting from feeling secure and confident to feeling insecure and lacking in confidence (Strasser, 1999), a state which often compels us to want to know, or in some unspecified manner to control, something in our lives in order not to feel the anxiety.

All emotions and associated anxieties can be useful when exploring clients' value systems and behaviour patterns. In fact, one of the shortest routes to a client's recognition of a way of being is through the clarification of their experience of anxiety. As discussed in previous chapters in which we explored the notion and process of freedom, anxiety can be our ally, our call to conscience to acknowledge issues that we may be evading or to which we are not responding.

Anxiety is both the everyday response to what occurs and is connected to the ontological hum, relating to the often uncomfortable, unsettling, and anxiety-provoking place which we inhabit. This discomfort stems from the bigger, often unanswerable questions about life and living, such as how to make meaning in a world that has no inherent meaning; how to make choices when there is no certainty to their outcome; how to make sense of the seemingly unresolvable paradoxes; and how to live in hope when we know we are going to die at a time that is usually not of our choosing. Although these ontological or life concerns are at the heart of existential thinking, the expression of anxiety usually manifests as depression, anxiety stress, panic attacks, sleeplessness and so on.

Existentialist philosophy acknowledges that living is unknown and unpredictable. 'To venture causes anxiety, but not to venture is to lose oneself' (Kierkegaard, 1941, p. 52). From this premise of uncertainty, existentialism tries to explore how people go about living within this kind of world.

From an existential perspective, anxiety can be understood as being a by-product of freedom and is natural, human and something not to be denied or eliminated. Integrated into the Wheel of Existence, anxiety becomes identifiable and can thus be described and understood. Often when we explore these existential givens with clients, they can integrate a new perspective, a new meaning into their worldview.

Despite – or perhaps in view of – our focus on creating a safe therapeutic environment for our clients, it is not the intention of the existential therapist to eliminate anxiety – an impossibility, in that anxiety is an existential 'given'. On the contrary, our goal is to create a safe enough environment for the tuning into, engagement with and exploration of anxiety.

The following case study shows how the Wheel of Existence can be used as a framework or backbone to elicit both ontological and ontic positions, interweaving the layers and leaves that pertain to the client's lived experience of anxiety.

> Leila overtly came to therapy to eliminate her anxiety. Her husband of over 20 years had decided that he no longer wanted to live with her, and her panic and despair were palpable. She couldn't sleep, she couldn't work and couldn't make sense of what had happened. The first few sessions were a torrent of tears intermingled with the story of her relationship. Leila had arrived in Australia at the age of 15 as a refugee from the Middle East. Similar to many refugees, her family were educated but their qualifications were not recognised by the Australian authorities and her father became a builder, eventually running his own small business. As the younger of two sisters, Leila was 'the good girl' – going to university, getting involved in her religious community, and getting married to a steady and reliable man. In contrast, her elder sister Nahir was deemed 'the naughty one' who created havoc at home and was of great concern to their parents.

Temporality and Uncertainty (Chapter 5)

The ontological givens – Temporality, discussed at length in Chapters 3, 4, and 5, and Uncertainty, described in Chapter 5 – create a perennial existential 'angst' that lurks in the back of the human mind.

> At an everyday level, Leila felt not only abandoned by Jeff, her husband, but rejected. Her sense of time and temporality was suspended. Everything she had come to believe about their past relationship and their future time together was unstuck. She didn't know what and whom to believe about whether Jeff was a good or bad person or whether it was her fault that he had left. Instead, she was wracked with her own sense of failure, believing that if she had been a better person, her husband would have stayed.
>
> Leila never thought that Jeff would leave. Although they had reached various impasses in their relationship, she 'knew' their marriage was forever. This is a good example of how the narrative we tell ourselves can keep us stuck in a past, fixed in the present, and clinging on to a future that will never happen. Time may not heal all wounds, but it certainly brings about shifts in perspectives. As our sessions progressed, Leila's feelings of panic and despair began to be interspersed with substantial self-reflections. Although she still felt Jeff's rejection, she was beginning to see how he might have felt rebuffed by her and that they were both at a time in their lives where they might want to pursue other and different kinds of sexual relationships.
>
> Although we had no agreement about the duration of therapy, there was an implicit urgency for Leila to get everything under control so she could return

to her less anxious and more containing existence. This urgency became less frantic as she began to own or take more responsibility for her part in their relationship. There was a visible inward, calming shift as she learnt to stay with and lean into her anxiety as her 'teacher'.

Revealing the Relationship and Establishing Safety
(Chapters 9 and 7)

During the first few weeks of our work together, Leila had been so overwhelmed at the end of our sessions that she had found it impossible to rise from her chair, asking to stay a little longer until she could gather herself. On both occasions, I remained seated and took her through a few rounds of deep breathing until she was calm enough to leave.

During our fourth session, I realised that I was anxious. I kept glancing at my watch, wondering how to keep Leila from experiencing a sudden panic as it dawned on her that it was time for our session to finish.

My anxiety was caused, first, by the fact that I had another client scheduled and was unsure about what would happen if they met. And I was also genuinely concerned at her distress. By noticing my anxiety and the story that I was telling myself, I realised that I didn't want to be another person in Leila's life who might reignite her feelings of self-loathing. I didn't want to be the betrayer, the next person to abandon her.

It appeared that Leila didn't want to leave the safety of my room and confront the reality of the world outside. She described her somatic response as 'an internal shaking' and fear, caused by the image of walking out into the empty and unknowing space. In our fifth session, we talked about how her panic attacks occurred at times when she felt the prickliness of abandonment. The trigger was usually around something Jeff had said or not said and the consequent feeling of being discarded and of no importance to him or anyone. It seemed that she was re-experiencing a version of this with me when I reminded her of the impending end of our session. As we talked about this, Leila became aware that in order to feel calmer it was necessary to talk to someone and had found a friend that was willing to be her listening ear. She also requested an extension of 10 minutes to our session time. There were no more panic attacks in our sessions, and she described the significance of feeling not only heard and supported but of having her request accepted.

Clarifying the Worldview (Chapter 11)

> Leila's worldview was tied up with being the watcher, the carer of her mother, so as never to be in trouble, and to guarantee that she did not become a burden to her mother. She witnessed the anxiety that her mother endured when her sister was detained at school or was absent from home. Unlike Leila, Nahir was uninterested in school and enjoyed what were deemed as dangerous activities in her country of origin. Her mother told Leila that she trusted her to be her eyes and ears and to keep Nahir out of trouble. These words spoken by her mother were not only significant to Leila as a child but continued to inhabit her sense of self throughout her adult life.

Choice (Chapters 5 and 13)

If we accept the explanation that our worldview is an existential phenomenon that we create to feel grounded and secure, it is also true that to move away from its inherent values and beliefs will create uncertainty and insecurity and may generate feelings of anxiety. A great deal of time is spent fearfully imagining a future that will rarely happen, so we often make fear-based choices in order to keep ourselves safe.

> Existentially, we are always in the hum of choosing, whether this be in our awareness or not. Leila chose to be the dutiful, good daughter in her attempt to keep her mother happy. It made her anxious, uncertain, and confused when this choice didn't have the desired effect of soothing her mother. She became aware of this mode of being, this worldview, during therapy and it became a useful comparison to refer to, as her story unfolded.

Clarifying the Worldview and Working with Paradox and Polarities (Chapters 11 and 12)

Our values and beliefs connect with our desire to have certainty, to have 'something' that gives us a sense of solidness, a secure sense and security that life is more than an ephemeral blip on our landscape of being. It also helps when we get praised or rewarded for the behaviours that are connected to our worldview. So for Leila, her sedimented belief or principle was to be a good girl, which included obeying all the implicit and explicit rules of her religion and family. Her reward was that she was her mother's confidante, a role which enabled her to prevent her mother feeling distressed and further reinforced her positive perception of herself as 'a good girl'.

We can get so accustomed to our anxiety that it can become entwined with our identity. Our anxiety can become sedimented. Sartre explained that the paradoxical and cyclical nature of bad faith binds us, through our anxiety, to who we believe we are in our entirety. We become adept at manipulating our circumstances to fit the person we believe we are and thus continue to live in bad faith. Yet, in our state of bad faith there is an inkling of 'something' that is slightly out of awareness, a vague recognition that recognises our pretence. Hence, we are anxious both when we deny our being as well as when we confront it.

> In her worldview, Leila did everything she could to ensure that she both felt that she was doing the right thing and – of equal importance – that she was seen as good by others. She also associated her role as that of a saviour and there were times when she felt superior to others. As a small child she remembers telling herself not to cry so as not to upset her mother. She learnt not to speak her truth in case it offended people. Her essential anxiety was that if she was a burden to others, they would die and she would be left alone and abandoned.
>
> It took several weeks for Leila to realise that her concept of not being a burden meant that she distanced herself from others and that this had potentially contributed to her husband's departure. In hindsight, he had often complained that he felt useless in their relationship, eventually spending time socialising with his friends rather than spending time with his wife.

Simply put, Leila's opposite position, or polarity, to being good and a saviour was her fear of being naughty and a burden to others. This is the black-and-white fixed position of a sedimentation where both positions are true, each requiring the opposite stance in order to flourish. Through an existential lens, this seemingly contradictory worldview is viewed as a paradox. Jaspers calls these 'anti-nomies' and claims, 'they are not resolved but only exacerbated . . . solutions can only be finite . . . while a look at the whole will always show the limiting insolubilities' (Jaspers, 1932, p. 218).

> By reflecting on the negative and positive qualities of both positions, Leila began to shift her relationship to her sedimented sense of self. Anxiety is a provocation and can reveal possibilities. Sometimes, exploring the polarity brings about a sense of calm, almost a 'coming home' to an aspect of oneself

> that has been denied for too long. Such exploration allowed Leila to realise that she could have an opinion without being a burden and that it could have a positive outcome. It was a relief not to have to be 'good' all the time. Therapy helped Leila see her anxiety as a provocation and that it could reveal possibilities.

Mood (Chapter 5)

As Heidegger notes in his writings about ontological givens, we are always in a mood. Our mood discloses how we are currently tuned into the world around us and shapes our perspective in that we can view the same story from differing standpoints. Moods can both open us up to alternative ways of seeing or close us off and limit our perspective.

When Leila first arrived in therapy, her anxious mood attuned her to being fearful of most people around her. She felt safest tucked away in her candle-lit bathroom. Moods can shift from moment to moment, so, like all of us, it didn't take much for Leila to swing from an enquiring, reflective mood to her anxious mood if a situation or conversation triggered her. Everything is interrelational, so the way in which we pay attention to the world changes what we find there, and what we find there changes the attention we pay to it. Our mood adjusts to this ebb and flow of life.

Our emotions are intertwined with our mood and are also a constant. We are never without an emotion. Freddie Strasser (1997) reminds us that our worldview, which is inclusive of our mood, reveals our emotions, and vice versa. Our emotional response gives us clues about our worldview, as was the case when Leila described her anxiety. In the break-up she was left bereft not only in the physical abandonment by her husband but also by the gaping feeling that she must have hurt or burdened Jeff, and therefore negated her worldview of being 'good' and 'a saviour'.

Integrating Mind and Body (Chapter 14)

> Leila often described herself as feeling small. Although she was small in stature, she was referring to her desire not to be seen in case she was seen to be a burden by others. This was juxtaposed to her paradoxical wish to be noticed and admired as someone who could save others.
>
> As Leila spoke she was also experiencing her feelings about herself and others. The existential view is that there no split between our mind and body

> but an intertwining of both, in that we take on experiences and feelings through our body as our body simultaneously reacts and responds to the experience. This idea equates to thinking and feeling through our bodies, which offers us information about other parts of ourselves and which Gendlin (1978) referred to as 'experiencing'.
>
> It was natural for Leila to focus in on her 'bodyhood' (Merleau-Ponty, 1962) or felt sense of events to help her elucidate her feelings. She recognised the dread, which she experienced as a sinking pit in her stomach on waking in the morning, which she was able to link to childhood events that were not only connected to her personal world, where being good and keeping her mother safe were paramount to her sense of wellbeing, but also to the bigger political situation of that era in the Middle East, where the reality of potential imprisonment and death pervaded her family's household.
>
> These connections helped Leila recognise that, in comparison to that era, she was reasonably safe. She began to make small but significant changes, such as leaving the light off at night and discovering that she could contradict her work colleagues and still be acknowledged for her ideas.

Facticity (Chapter 5)

It is sometimes difficult for clients to accept that there are limitations to their living and existence. They haven't come to terms with their facticity, the innate characteristics such as our height, colour, DNA, race, nationality, and so forth that we cannot change. Many believe that their path to happiness lies in eliminating anxieties. Yet, adopting this attitude can lead clients along a false path where they expect that strategies such as positive doing and thinking, or becoming more assertive, will accomplish happiness. If and when they realise that, in spite of all these efforts, they can still fail, the primary existential fear and anxiety take on a different nature, creating a self-perpetuating loop of anxiety. The fear thus becomes fear of the fear, and anxiety, anxiety of the anxiety.

Only when Leila accepted that there were valid reasons for Jeff's departure, and understood that life has its limitations, could she choose how she saw herself, how she reacted to Jeff and how she perceived their relationship as a whole. She became aware that she need not become totally frustrated by not being the 'ideal', good, caring person who would live without obstacles and anxiety, but she had the choice of accepting these and herself as a reality; she could choose different pathways. Anxiety was not the enemy that she had initially feared.

Working with Paradox and Polarities and Exploring the Four Worlds (Chapters 12 and 10)

Yalom (1980), in his key text *Existential Psychotherapy*, highlighted four defences or concerns that arise from existential anxiety: those of death, freedom, existential isolation, and meaninglessness. I find that by my bearing these four concerns in mind, I can help deepen clients' connections to their anxieties, anxieties which are bound up with the ultimate paradoxes that we humans have to face: learning to live a full life, with the knowledge that we are going to die; understanding that our freedom is limited; that even though we are always in relationship, we are ultimately alone; and appreciating that to thrive, we need to create meaning and purpose against the backdrop that life is inherently without meaning.

Once again, when exploring our anxieties, these four existential concerns are interconnected with each other as well as to all the 'leaves' of the Wheel of Existence.

In his book *Staring at the Sun* (2008), Yalom emphasises how our denial of our mortality is pervasive and obstructs our freedom. Denial of death is not only inauthentic but, as Rollo May wrote, it is 'self-alienation' (1961) since awareness of finitude gives significance to living.

> In her childhood, Leila lived with a constant hum of death and loss of freedom in all her Four Worlds – the physical, social, private, and spiritual (as will be described in Chapter 9). She lived in a country where her community's religion was seen as the work of the devil and she experienced constant discrimination at school and amongst her peers who were told not to befriend her. As a child, Leila would not have described herself as anxious, until arriving in Australia where, comparing herself to other people, she began to wonder about some of her routine habits. Sleeping with the light on, experiencing vivid dreams of escaping from various enemies, having few friends, and even questioning her religious upbringing were all themes for exploration in therapy.

Identifying Choices and Meaning (Chapter 13)

> In her mind, Leila had always imagined herself as married to Jeff and one of two parents to their children. This picture of herself gave her meaning. Although their relationship had previously on several occasions broken down, Leila had never thought they would separate. She was scared to imagine herself as a single person, as potentially facing life on her own. Loneliness and meaninglessness were entwined as inverse to being in a relationship and

> deriving meaning. As Leila's anxiety settled, she could see that her previous life had been satisfactory but also quite closed. She had made choices to keep the family intact and now she could glimpse other possibilities.

Time and Endings (Chapters 3 and Chapter 4)

For the first few weeks, much of Leila's therapy concentrated on the ending of her relationship with Jeff. During this phase of therapy, she was in a high state of anxiety that increased immeasurably as the realisation dawned that Jeff was not returning. Leila felt that the world she knew and her identity as a mother, wife, and companion had come to an end, and she didn't feel she had the inner resources to build a new world.

The rejection she experienced felt like an ultimate elimination of self, so it was hard to introduce the idea that our time together would also end. It is here that the philosophical stance of existential therapy comes to the fore in that it is a universal given that everything inevitably finishes. Although there was no overt agreement on the precise number of sessions, we spoke about her desire to pursue other forms of self-development when her immediate crisis was alleviated. She had come to therapy wanting to be nurtured through her crisis and, once over, she saw this juncture as a natural end. Anxiety was still a feature of Leila's life and she was concerned about how to juggle her time and finances, but it was an anxiety that had movement, that would take her into the future, and so the ending of therapy mirrored this forward passage of time.

In line with life's uncertainty, another unexpected event changed the path of our therapy: I decided to move my therapy room. My new room was smaller and more intimate, and Leila found the move and the different space hard to handle. She spoke as if the old space was trustworthy but that in the new room she had to start again. There was too little space and she felt under closer scrutiny. Her time with me came to an end and we parted, earlier than I anticipated and sooner that I had hoped. On this occasion, it was I as the therapist that had to come to terms with an unwished-for ending and what it meant to me. For Leila, the initial crisis was over, and she had reached a calmer equilibrium.

Understanding Authenticity (Chapter 15)

Without anxiety, we would remain static, unable to move forward and unable to take responsibility for ourselves. For some people, anxiety is crippling, and it renders them immobile. It feels as if their relationship to their anxiety, their ontic experience of anxiety, locks them into closed self-perpetuating loops.

On the other hand, Leila was a good example of how anxiety can be a 'teacher', if we are courageous enough to stay with the upheaval it generates. Heidegger (1962) writes about this process of developing a sense of self-awareness, the path towards authenticity, as a process of *becoming*. Sartre (1958) writes about 'good faith' as the 'owning' of our position in life, when we take up the mantle of responsibility and can act from this place of authentic identity. And Spinelli writes about the state of 'verb-ing' where 'our existence is a dynamic, continuous becoming' (2015, p. 60).

Clients will often embark on therapy when they 'hear' or feel a 'call to consciousness'. The therapy relationship provides them with a 'reality check', facilitating a process whereby they will be offered support to examine and embrace their lives in all their fluctuating twists and turns. As we become more aware, we are offered an opportunity to create a new sense of ourselves.

9

Revealing the Relationship

I have almost invariably found that the very feeling which has seemed to me most private, most personal, and hence most incomprehensible by others, has turned out to be an expression for which there is a resonance in many other people. It has led me to believe that what is most personal and unique in each one of us is probably the very element which would, if it were shared or expressed, speak most deeply to others.

Carl Rogers, *On Becoming a Person* (1961)

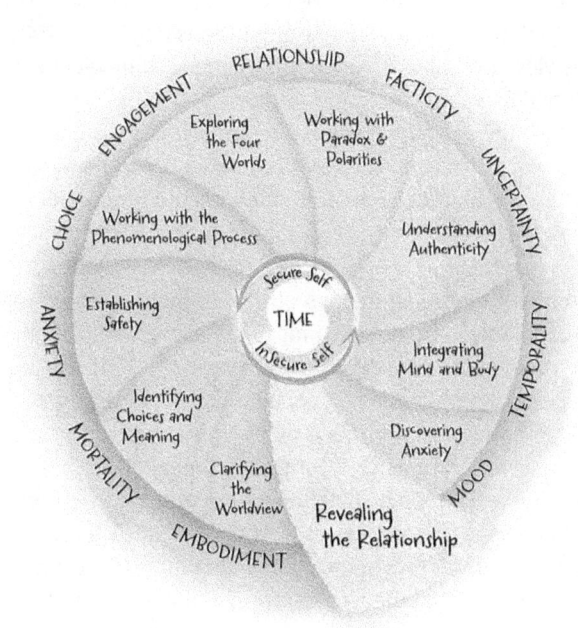

Source: Alison Strasser

Time-Limited Existential Therapy: The Wheel of Existence, Second Edition. Alison Strasser.
© 2022 John Wiley & Sons Ltd. Published 2022 by John Wiley & Sons Ltd.

As an ontological given, *relationship* was described in Chapter 5 as a universal experience of being-in-the-world. In therapy, the relationship is viewed both as an ontological given, in that relatedness is inevitable, and as an ontic response, in that the manner of our relating is interpersonal and specific to each relationship, as well as a feature that is integral to the therapeutic process.

The key components of the phenomenological process, discussed in Chapter 6 – the art of questioning and interpretation, the attitude of un-knowing and the inclusivity of the dialogic stance – are also integral to maintaining a spirit of relatedness in the practice of existential therapy.

This chapter will explore how our styles of relating are revealed through our various unique relational patterns, our ontic response.

The existential view argues that the self is not a discrete entity but is always a 'self in relation', in that we live permanently in relationship with others. There is no individual or self without others, no solo silo without the context of society and culture at large. There is no self without a view of another person in our mind's eye. As such, the themes of responsibility, freedom and choice are not statements that revolve around the individual's needs and concerns but are in constant relation to the many 'others', both seen and unseen, that inhabit our lives. Hence, 'no choice can be mine or yours alone, no experienced impact of choice can be separated in terms of "my responsibility" versus "your responsibility", no sense of personal freedom can truly avoid its interpersonal dimensions' (Spinelli, 2001, pp. 15–16). This relational view is central to existential/phenomenological psychotherapy, the practice of which was explored in Chapter 4.

Significant to understanding the existential view of relationship is the concept of *intentionality* – a strange word, but one that describes how human beings are always connected to other people, objects, ideas, and phenomena. Intentionality, literally, is our intention towards something and it imbues how we both experience and act in the world.

Life is replete with different kinds of relationships, each with their own patterns of communication. As we come into contact with a range of people, we adapt and learn different styles of relating which include different levels of self-disclosure. We reveal ourselves in different ways; we can be open and honest, declaring ourselves freely – authentically, in existential terms – or we can be inauthentic in relationships, concealing ourselves, hiding our feelings and thoughts. The stance we choose will depend on our relationship history, the nature of the current relational encounter, the level and type of trust and how much we need to protect ourselves. We can, however, only disclose what we know about ourselves within our own current limits of experience. In other words, we can only know what we know, and what we don't know, we don't!

Terms such as *reflective* or *unreflective*, even *pre-reflective* (Sartre, 1958), or *awareness* and *non-awareness*, are used to describe our capacity for self-awareness.

Therapy becomes a facilitation of 'unreflective emotions that emerge into reflective ones' (Strasser, 1999, p. 27) and in so doing, expands our experience so that alternative or additional versions of our stories are revealed.

> To approach the **Other** in **conversation** is to welcome his expression, in which at each instant he overflows the idea a thought would carry away from it. It is therefore to **receive from the Other** beyond the capacity of the I, which means exactly: to have the idea of infinity. But this also means: to be taught. (Levinas, 1998, p. 51)

The Interrelational Relationship

In existential therapy, as with all therapies, there are moments where client and therapist experience a feeling of 'togetherness'. These are when the therapist experiences an intense understanding of how the client gains his or her meaning, when there is a confluence of two understanding minds working towards the greater whole. It does require the therapist to hold and to reveal, both to themselves and potentially to their clients, their personal experience of being with their client. It is not enough to only respond to a client's experience through empathic attunement; at certain moments it will be helpful to add some content around the 'I' of the therapist's experience.

Heidegger (1962) views all human beings as connected to each other or *being-with-others*, the hyphens denoting this intrinsic connectivity. Current views of psychotherapy refer to this as 'the interrelationship'.

Martin Buber and Carl Rogers, in the mid-twentieth century, are probably the first therapists to work with a position of the interpersonal (rather than intrapsychic) relationship. Buber (1970) proposed that there is no 'I' in isolation and argued that this relational position is experienced through two basic modes of relating. The *I–It* mode essentially treats the other as an Object, as an extension of personal needs, even if offered with warmth and caring. An *I–Thou* mode of relating, conversely, is one of 'inclusion', where there is a total awareness of the other while still retaining one's personal identity. Both forms of relating serve a purpose and are evident in the therapeutic relationship.

Emmy van Deurzen (2012) writes about the ideal relationship, which she calls the 'I–Me' relationship. Although by and large utopian, this 'I–Me' formulation, she suggests, is the perfect 'fantasy' relationship. Generally unattainable, the 'I–Me' structure allows us to understand the elements for which we, as humans, strive, as an ideal. She writes that in this type of relationship is 'the perfect merging of two beings who totally identify with each other and who operate in absolute self-forgetfulness, aiming at something that transcends their separateness and thus binds them together' (2012, p. 213). Some people might fantasise about this kind of relationship, some may comfortably surrender to the fusion, while others would find it suffocating.

> Bob often felt disregarded by others and knew that he was experienced by them as angry and frightening. He didn't like his anger but felt it was at least one way of expressing his discontent at the way in which other people treated him. When I expressed that I too felt 'cast aside' at his tendency to brush over my comments and insist that his view was right, Bob's tone softened and we were able explore his ontic 'I–It' relational style. He noticed that he had difficulty tolerating people when they had differing ideas to his own or when they disagreed with him, and that he felt rejected and cast aside (as I had) when he felt he hadn't been heard. This realisation was followed by sadness. In that moment, Bob was able to find and experience a more authentic way of being in relationship with me.

Heidegger (1962) makes a distinction between a rational, calculative type of conversation which can objectify and dominate a relationship, and an intuitive, meditative type of conversation where dialogue is based on respect, loving, and an openness to holding the un-knowing, allowing for the awe of mystery.

Sartre, on the other hand, describes how we only become aware of ourselves through the 'look' and the 'gaze' of others:

> The gaze that I encounter . . . is not a seen gaze [that is, not an eye that I see looking at me] but a gaze imagined by me in the field of the Other . . . the sound of rustling leaves heard while out hunting . . . a footstep heard in a corridor . . . [The gaze exists] not at the level of [a particular visible] other whose gaze surprises the subject looking through the keyhole. It is that the other surprises him, the subject, as entirely hidden gaze. (Sartre in Lacan, 1998, p. 84)

This gaze, whether real or imagined, evokes a range of feelings including shame, fear, care, loving, liking, hatred, guilt. We sense ourselves being observed and tend to take on some of the characteristics projected onto us. Juggling others' perceptions of us is complex, as we can see with Bob. Therapy is also a process of dissecting and reconstructing a sense of self that can take into account the self that others have construed about us, balanced with the reality of who we are and our own desires for the self that we want.

> Annabel, a supervisee, announced how she adored her client, Paul. Considering her statement further, Annabel depicted Paul as reminiscent of her younger brother who she also idealised and who could do no wrong. My probing questions were intended to broaden Annabel's perspective, and before the end of our supervision session she realised that she had placed Paul on a pedestal, not taking into consideration how he often cancelled appointments at the last moment and frequently forgot to pay for them. The next time we met, Annabel excitedly related how the previous supervision had shifted her 'gaze', allowing her to see Paul in greater breadth. Significantly, Annabel's shift caused an ontic response in Paul; he had felt the change in Annabel's attitude, breathing a sigh of relief that he no longer had to be the 'golden' boy and could now talk about his mischievous behaviour and other depravities. As Annabel appreciated Paul in his entirety and saw him as his own Subject, he could now take up his own mantle, regaining authorship and authenticity. Annabel too was changed by the encounter, shocked by how easy it was to hold the other in one's gaze, influencing and restricting their mode of being.

Carl Rogers, creator of the client-centred approach, wrote about the facilitative attitude that primarily and commonly consists of three elements: congruence, unconditional positive regard, and empathy. In short, a caring, congruent relationship creates a particular specialness in the therapeutic encounter. From these, clients can grow in a constructive manner when 'there is a close matching, or congruence, between what is being experienced at the gut level, and what is present in awareness, and what is expressed to the client' (Rogers, 1980, p. 115).

There are many overlaps between the person-centred and existential positions, one being the significance of the therapeutic relationship and what occurs between two people when there is a 'meeting' or I/Thou encounter (Buber, 1970). Such 'meeting', also known as 'presence', can be described as a moving towards and immersion of both the therapist and client. It is when a feeling of connection and groundedness emerges, an overall sense of being understood and not judged.

While different authors have different views about the purpose of this relational mode of working in a therapeutic situation, all of them would converge in accepting the premise that through this interpersonal mode, whether we call it *togetherness* (Sartre, 1957), *I–Thou* (Buber, 1970) or *moments of meeting* (Stern, 2004), one can promote a change in clients' perceptions:

> it means that something you said truly impacts on me and changes me: it doesn't just act as an opening for me to say what I was always planning to say – it doesn't simply alter my trajectory; it becomes part of my being. (Cooper & Spinelli, 2012, p. 146)

The Four Relationship Realms

Working relationally from the existential position is inclusive of all of the above and it can be helpful to further understand the complexity of relationships by breaking it down into four perspectives or realms of encounter, namely: self-to-self (I), self-to-other (You), self-with-other (We), and self-with-world (They).

As with most existential ideas, we flow in and out of these realms, non-sequentially, depending on our current sense of self, the relationship we're encountering and the external circumstances occurring in any given moment. These realms also take into account our perception of others as well as the person's relationship with their prevailing environment (Spinelli, 1989, 2006). Each of these realms of encounter exist in every meeting and, as such, are helpful when exploring how we exist in our relationships. In the therapeutic encounter, a conversation where both the therapist and client talk about their sense of self in relation to the other, and vice versa, has the potential not only to add a richness to the encounter but also to be expressive of those inner values and beliefs that propel us into action.

Self-to-Self

As we listen to our clients, we may find ourselves simultaneously reflecting on our own issues, taking into account our personal experiences, our current mood, and sense of being, wondering about our capacity to listen deeply as we become aware of preconceived ideas and feelings. Our awareness enables us to bracket our biases, following the phenomenological ideal. In other words, as I experience myself with my client I too am aware of myself as the therapist reacting to the client. The client, too, will be reacting to the therapist. Spinelli (2007) describes this as the 'self-to-self' or 'I-focused' realm of encounter.

> Prior to our meeting for the first time, Justine had negotiated six sessions. I immediately liked her. She was attractive and upbeat with a certain strength in her. I experienced her openness in her wanting to understand more about her marriage and her experience of feeling second rate when her partner fell in love with another woman. They had agreed to an 'open relationship', each giving the other permission to have sex with other partners. Throughout their marriage, Alex had slept with other women but never fallen in love. As Justine spoke, I became aware of how I was feeling; I wished to be seen by Justine as open and approachable. I was afraid that Justine would see me as prim and prudish. Was I flexible enough to embrace their sexual arrangement? Listening

> more carefully, I realised that Justine was also confused by the tension between her desire to embrace Alex's sexual liaisons and her feelings of rejection and inferiority as a woman. I could feel her conflict and relate to her confusion, an example of the I-focused realm.
>
> Justine believed that their relationship counsellor had referred her to me because she had personal issues to resolve. The inference that Justine understood from this was that she had become the problem, because Alex had kept to their deal and was open and transparent about his love for both women, and that Justine should accept this previously agreed upon arrangement.
>
> In the third of the six sessions, and in a fine example of the I-focused realm, Justine mused over the question, 'Who am I?' noticing that she could view herself in various roles: as the compliant, lady-in-waiting; as the observer, who watches and notices; as the mediator who smooths over other people's problems; as the angry, petulant Justine who has tantrums when nobody is watching.

Self-to-Other

The self-to-other or 'you-focused realm of encounter' (Spinelli, 2007) describes the phase of relating when a picture of how the therapist reacts to their client, or vice versa, emerges. Essentially, it's how I imagine you (the other) sees me.

This might include a range of responses such as boredom, anticipation, trust, lack of trust, liking or disliking the client. It also embraces other perceptions and observations, such as how the therapist experiences the client's reactions to interventions or how the therapist imagines the client experiences the therapist, my experience of the client as a 'you', or the client experiencing the therapist as a 'you' and their imagined sense of 'you'. Often neglected, but of great importance, is when the therapist reveals their experience of being *with* their client *to* the client or in supervision. Even if not said to the client, it is a crucial requirement that in supervision the therapist reflects on their experience of the client. Questions to oneself such as: how do you feel about your client? how do you experience your client? what do you imagine they say about you? all help to inform the therapist about the client's overall self-to-other impact in relationship.

In answering these questions in supervision about Justine, I experienced both her deference in relation to me and also her strength in the way she negotiated the six sessions. I experienced how I was both drawn towards her and then felt pushed away. I contemplated in supervision whether she might feel a similar experience?

> As I learnt more about Justine, I noticed that this push/pull feeling was evident in her other relationships. Justine appeared a strong and influential person with her children, friends, and work colleagues. Conversely, I sometimes experienced her as unsure or even subordinate in the way she spoke about herself in terms of some aspects of her marriage. She had met Alex, a more mature man, as a young girl when she had moved from the country to live in Sydney. It was the late 1970s and an era of sexual experimentation. In a striking parallel to my fear of being seen by Justine as prim and prudish, Justine too had not wanted Alex to see her as old-fashioned and convinced herself that she too wanted an open marriage. It was important for Justine to be liked and accepted by others, including me. Even though at times she was upset or cried during the session, it felt significant that she would always leave composed, saying something positive about the session or me. Justine wanted to be seen as strong and independent, not as someone who was needy and vulnerable. She wanted to be optimistic; she wanted to see her relationship with her husband and myself as positive and, similarly, to achieve a positive outcome in her therapy. In essence, if Justine could remain accepting of Alex's lifestyle, she felt this positive acceptance would be reciprocated. As an intermingling of the You and I focus, Justine was imagining how Alex saw her (You-focus) and adjusted her sense of I-focus to accommodate his perception.

Self-with-Other

The third aspect that occurs in all relationships is, the 'We-focused realm of encounter' (Spinelli, 2007). In this realm of relationship, the focus remains with our immediate interrelationships or being 'with' the other. This realm of encounter may incorporate elements of Sartre's *gaze*, Heidegger's description of *being-with* the other in an intuitive, meditative conversation, shrouded in an *awe of mystery*, Stern's *moments of meeting*, Buber's *I–Thou*, van Deurzen's *I–Me* and Rogers' caring, empathic, and congruent relationship.

In the clinical setting, the therapeutic task is to explore what emerges from the interaction between client and therapist, between the first two realms of relationship, and our sense of being-in-relationship with the client. The client too relates their experience of being-with-the-therapist both implicitly and explicitly to the therapist. This exploration may illuminate problems or issues occurring in the 'in-between' of therapist and client.

> Justine had never thought about trust, she had merely assumed it was intrinsic to all her close relationships. As we talked, she realised that she didn't trust as transparently as she had imagined. It was more that she was *supposed* to trust,

> it was a belief, which had now been shaken by Alex falling in love with another woman. Through the process of therapy, she realised too that she had never fully trusted anyone. Her mother had been mentally unstable, her siblings were unreliable and her father, whom she had adored, on dying had left his estate to her brothers.

So how were we both experiencing 'us being in relation with another' (Spinelli, 2015, p. 187)? Following her revelation about distrusting others, I tentatively broached this question with Justine by admitting 'that I felt that we both liked each other but were not sure how to trust each other?'

> Justine admitted that she had been circumspect about what she talked about because she was afraid that she would collapse emotionally and would then have to continue with therapy. She had her own time limit. It was more important to her to get on with her life and her relationship with Alex and to finish her therapy at the end of the following session. Therapy and her therapist represented 'yet another person in her life to please'. Once again, I was experiencing her push towards intimacy and the pulling away at the prospect of getting too close.

This was an example of how the issue of trust that emerged in the in-between of Justine and me was affecting both of us in quite different ways. We were both unsure of how to trust the other and, until we spoke about it, were each left with our personal musings of how each perceived the other. By bringing the topic of trust into the conversation, our picture of each other was enlarged and we emerged with a greater understanding of what trust meant for each of us. Concurrently, we were co-creating a different sense of trust in our relationship that could be spoken about and brought back into Justine's relationship with Alex.

If handled through honesty and genuine disclosure by both people, a particular mode of 'between-ness' can occur, sometimes described as *resonance* or *presence*. This meeting of two people is beyond words, where 'neither tries to enslave or be enslaved by the other' (van Deurzen, 2012, p. 213) and the experience of mutuality and respect is profound.

Working 'with' the therapeutic relationship, 'within' the therapeutic relationship and with the client's intrinsic experience of relationships reveals the full gamut of the client's relational world. We are inextricably linked to all others, whether in actual meeting or in our imagination. Phenomenology describes how our sense of 'I', or who I believe I am (and therefore who I believe I am not), is interdependent with or contingent on how we imagine others perceive us. Hence 'no choice can be mine or yours alone, no experienced impact of choice can be separated in terms of "my responsibility" versus "your responsibility", no sense of personal freedom can truly avoid its interpersonal dimensions' (Spinelli, 2001, p. 16).

> In our sixth and final session, Justine admitted that Alex from the start of their relationship had influenced her. He set up her business, she moved into his house, and she had agreed to the 'open' relationship, which he had instigated. Now, she wasn't so sure. She had grown up believing in monogamy but hadn't questioned how the life she was living contradicted this value. In response to my observations about my experience of us and how she had come with a very clear idea of what she had wanted from therapy and the number of sessions this would take, she also recognised her influence over Alex. Before their children moved to high school, she forced Alex away from his island sanctuary and into the heart of inner-city living. She dictated the home environment, and now she wondered about the impact of this on Alex.
>
> She had entered therapy with a 'poor me' stance: that Alex had broken their agreement by falling in love with another woman. She now had to face her own limitations, realising that her accommodating stance had also benefited her, and additionally she had influenced Alex to make changes and was much more in control of her life that she had admitted.

Self-with-World

Often forgotten but equally important is the fourth realm of every relationship (Spinelli, 2015), known as the 'They-focus', which includes the external world of the client's relationship, such as friends and work colleagues, as well as its overriding social and cultural factors. For instance, Justine and Alex's 'open relationship' was indicative of the particular social milieu and cultural environment of the late 1970s in Sydney. Justine moved into Alex's work and social milieu and assumed his lifestyle, which was a complete contrast to that of her family of origin in the depths of country Australia. She had grown up feeling constrained and different from her community and family, and in Alex she found an opportunity for apparent freedom.

Justine and I parted without her having a specific answer to how her relationship with Alex would evolve, but she was more open to seeing how her adaptation to the wishes of others might have compromised her own values. I too was touched by how much our beliefs concede to our pervading culture and our desire to conform.

It must be clear by now, that from an existential perspective the natural primordial state of human beings is that of 'being-in-the-world', an integral element of which is 'being-with-others' in this inseparable relationship with each other. As one of the intrinsic human 'givens', there is a mutual communion among people and a natural interdependence of human beings. We'll discuss being-in-the-world in greater depth in Chapter 10.

Various research projects now acknowledge that it is not the model of therapy or the techniques administered that have the greatest impact on the outcome of therapy, but the belief held by clients that change is possible (Duncan, Miller, Wampold, & Hubble, 2010) and the 'realness' of the relationship. How each client experiences each therapist will differ so that two people seeing the same therapist will have an entirely different encounter. 'The client you meet as the therapist is the client who meets you. There is no client *as such*. If two therapists meet the same client, it is not the same client' (Cohn, 1997, p. 33).

10

Exploring the Four Worlds

Our task is to be guide, friend, and interpreter to persons on their journeys through their private hells and purgatories.

Rollo May, *The Cry for Myth* (1991)

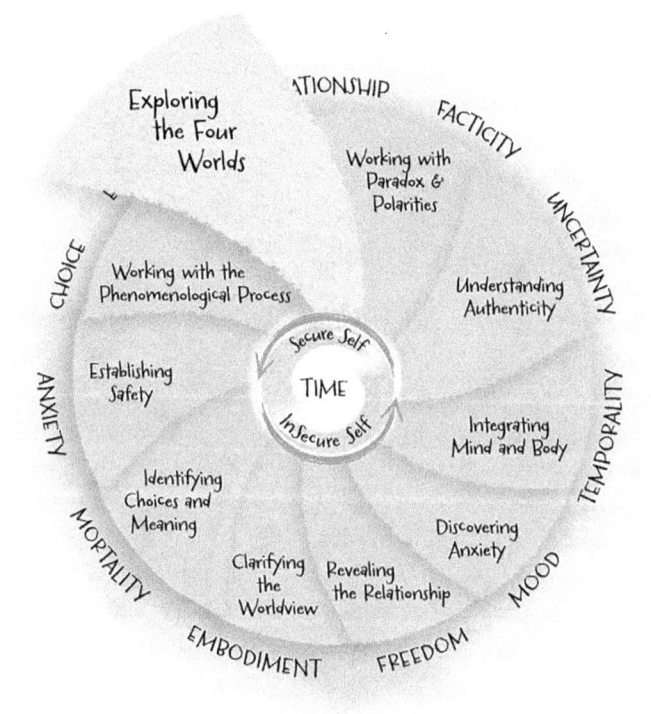

Source: Alison Strasser

Time-Limited Existential Therapy: The Wheel of Existence, Second Edition. Alison Strasser.
© 2022 John Wiley & Sons Ltd. Published 2022 by John Wiley & Sons Ltd.

This chapter, 'Exploring the Four Worlds', exemplifies the 'hyphens' of being-in-the-world highlighting the existential view of interconnectedness. If we take for example a specific personal principle, it can be tracked and understood in all the four worlds. Similarly, temporality and our relationship to time is revealed when we contemplate the physical, social, private, and spiritual worlds. In this way, time is mapped onto the four worlds and the four worlds are mapped onto time.

Ludwig Binswanger (1963), a Swiss psychiatrist and one of the first practitioners to integrate existential philosophy into his work with patients, showed how we could examine Heidegger's idea of being-in-the-world from three distinct but overlapping dimensions: the *Umwelt* (physical world), the *Mitwelt* (public world), and the *Eigenwelt* (private world). The fourth, the *Überwelt* (spiritual world), was added by van Deurzen (1988). These four dimensions

> provide a map of human existence on which an individual's position and trajectory can be plotted and understood. This allows the therapist to facilitate her client's journey through life and encourage her to expand and travel into new territories rather than restricting or limiting themselves.
> (van Deurzen, 2012, p. 75)

Umwelt

The *Umwelt* is the physical world, with its predetermined physical, biological, and instinctual dimension. In the dimension of time, our physical being is responding to its circadian rhythm in terms of sleep and waking cycles, the lunar phase, and other atmospheric conditions. It also includes our relationship to our body, our attitudes around health and wealth as well as our interactions with our surrounding environment such as climate, rural or city life, home setting, and so on.

At the level of the broader ontological hum, this physical world connects to time and temporality and to our relationship to death and dying as well as how we live our life. People with eating disorders usually have a very distorted view of their shape and size. The way in which they relate to their body shape can bring out different perspectives.

As discussed in Chapter 5, our physical appearance, our DNA, and possibly aspects of our personality are immutable. Hence it is also connected to the ontic givens such as facticity, engagement, and embodiment.

As one of the ontic givens, variations arise in the way each person relates to these different factors.

> Iris would oscillate between dark periods of depression and cheerful times of creative activity; the swings were linked to her grasping to find meaning. Her style of dress and posture would change significantly depending on her current mood. In therapy, she also brought out her relationship with her plants, which she either starved of water or tended to with love and care. Her therapy helped her to recognise that her treatment of her plants reflected how she felt towards herself.
>
> As Iris began to accept a slower pace and was less self-deprecating, her sense of dress and personal style emerged. Each week she would appear taller and more elegant.

Mitwelt

Our public or social world, the *Mitwelt*, pertains to the dimension of our everyday relationship to others and includes our attitudes towards social class, race, gender, culture, and the general rules of our particular society. It is also the world of our everyday encounters with other people, the way we interact socially with others.

Some key points that might emerge are the ways that clients cope with other people: do they automatically take a like or dislike to people, do they only accept people whom they perceive as having the same views as themselves, do they want to be in control of their relationships, do they prefer to be submissive? These are all aspects of the *Mitwelt* that the therapist can explore with the client in order to clarify his or her attitudes towards these various aspects of society at large.

> Patrick valued his independence since he equated its polarity, dependence, with neediness and therefore considered it a weakness. In his social world of friendships he enjoyed the company of others who were fun-loving, and independent. Yet, in his sexual world Patrick adamantly wanted his partners to be gregarious and autonomous and, paradoxically, also reliant on him. He would insist on paying for meals and any other expenses incurred on a night out. When the contradiction of wanting his sexual partners to be both independent of and dependent on him was highlighted, Patrick realised that he only felt in control when his partners were in need of him. This preference also gives us a clue about his manner of relating to others, as depicted in the Revealing the Relationship leaf on the Wheel of Existence.

The *Mitwelt* or social world reveals our experience of belonging or feelings of isolation and sense of being different from or aligned to others. At an emotional level, it's the link to how we react to others in terms of feeling rejected or accepted by them. These reactions will vary, as with Patrick, according to different social settings. Patrick's differing ways of relating fit neatly into the three ways of interacting with other people in the *Mitwelt*: dominance over, submission to or withdrawal from the situation (van Deurzen, 2012, p. 85). These relational patterns emanate from the idea that people are inherently competitive. However, the fourth way of relating is that of cooperation and inclusion. Sometimes within one exchange the mode will shift and change and will vary, too, as with Patrick in his interactions with different people.

> In Louise's case, her professional life as a lawyer included everyday interactions with colleagues and clients that were based within the three modes described above, in a relatively balanced way. However, her home life was in complete contrast in that she was subject to both verbal and physical abuse by her husband. She was largely submissive to his needs in the hope that she could keep their relationship on an even keel. It was not until Louise could recognise the contrast and the imbalance in her relationships, both at the office and at home, that she could begin to work on herself.

Within the social dimension, time and temporality reveals itself in various actions including how we schedule our days and nights, how we respond and create routines, and how we negotiate our arrival for prearranged meetings. These ontic reactions overlap with the other three worlds and are responses to our foreknowledge that everything has an end.

> Since a small child, Luke was adamant he had to be punctual and would get anxious when his mother dilly-dallied around the house rather than leave to get to their destination on time. His concern was that he would miss out on whatever might be happening whether at school, with friends and, later in life, at work. He remembers as a child his first encounter with death, when a close family member contracted cancer and seemed to shrink in front of his eyes, going from an energetic and fun person to a decaying, old woman. This experience of a loved one's process of dying filled Luke with fear and trepidation, unable to comprehend how life can end so abruptly. Once this connection to time, being late and death was revealed, the therapy conversations turned to the subject of dying and all the unreflected anxieties he had internalised and embodied.

Eigenwelt

The third dimension, *Eigenwelt*, is the private, intimate world of the client. This is the space of both the intimate relationship that one has with oneself, as well as the relationship one has with significant others. It is the 'I' of our inner world, with our sense of how we understand ourselves as connected to our self-esteem, levels of confidence and view of ourselves. Included are our thoughts, feelings, values, and ideas that add up to our personal sense of identity. It is the dimension where our values and beliefs about oneself and our relationship to others come to the fore. Our self-esteem and sense of who we believe we are (and are not) is allied to how we react to situations in terms of feeling successful or believing that we are a failure.

In therapy, the *Eigenwelt* is where the client can tussle with their interpretations of their interactions with parents, siblings, friends, and authority figures, often emerging with a different perspective.

> As Clara began to see herself through the eyes of others and could admit to her competiveness, she began to notice that comments she had previously taken as criticisms were in fact not laden with any such negative implications. She began to notice that she didn't collapse when people made critical comments and, although she still heard the criticism, she could see the link to the specific issue raised, rather than feel the total annihilation of her sense of self. Relating this back to her worldview and sedimentation, she was beginning to find a more flexible stance towards herself. She embraced her competitiveness differently and indeed now used words like 'keenness' and 'determination' to describe herself and her actions.

Our relationship to time and temporality in this personal world reflects our internal sense of time and how we negotiate this with ourselves.

> Tess, an actress, hated the fact that she arrived late for her auditions, as she did for our weekly sessions. It was a topic that we constantly returned to as she wrestled with her sense of failure as an actress. At 31, Tess thought that she would never achieve the fame and glory she had wanted from childhood. Time was her enemy and metaphorically she was fighting it through her tardiness. She found it hard to accept that acting was a hard and ruthless profession, and each time she didn't get a role she had to endure her feelings of failure. Exploring the tension between fame and success and inconspicuousness and failure brought to light her yearning for the approval of her father

> who was elderly and in frail health. Tess was afraid that he would die before she achieved fame, leaving her deflated and feeling insignificant. I smile as I write this, remembering watching Tess on television acting in a significant role.

Überwelt

Finally, the *Überwelt*, or the meaning world, is concerned with a person's connection with life's meaning and purpose, with spiritual values as well as personal perspectives of living and dying. Often clients come to therapy when they have 'crisis of meaning', when it feels as if their world that helped give them structure and meaning has collapsed. Although clients would not necessarily define their crisis as that of the spiritual dimension, the *Überwelt* is the world where we define our purpose, explain our existence and create meaning for ourselves against the backdrop of a world without inherent meaning. In therapy, it 'means grasping how this person makes sense of the world and what it is she lives for and would be willing to die for' (van Deurzen, 2012, p. 103). What is it that gets us up in the morning? This could be a spirit of adventure, our engagement and a curiosity, a sense of what we can fashion for ourselves against the backdrop of life's limitations.

Simply put, existentialists believe that to live life more fully, our meaning is self-created. Even a religious person who takes his or her own particular meaning from religious texts may differ from someone else's sense of the same religion. People express their values through religion, not necessarily the other way around, and also through agnostic, even atheistic and other belief systems that are influenced by their cultural, social, and familial backgrounds.

Encompassing the *Überwelt* means to take into account the polarity. Within the world of meaning and purpose is that of lack of meaning or futility. Each of the worlds is connected to each of the others and relates back to the ontological givens.

> Laura came to therapy explicitly to explore purpose and meaning. Since childhood she had been searching and couldn't find anything that added value to her life. Every day was a struggle interspersed with moments of hope when she thought she might have discovered the ultimate purpose. Laura explored a range of religions, read philosophy, completed psychological tests on values, studied homeopathy, and worked in a variety of organisations from corporate to not-for-profit, imagining that she would find there the essential values she was searching for. I too was at a loss, feeling as directionless as Laura, until I recognised that she was looking for the impossible, the ideal, the answer to

> everything, as pronounced in *The Hitchhiker's Guide to the Galaxy*: 'The Answer to the Great Question... Of Life, the Universe and Everything... Is... Forty-two,' said Deep Thought, with infinite majesty and calm...' (Adams, 1975, p. 144)

Time and temporality in the spiritual dimension is concerned with our beliefs about what happens to us after we die and what constitutes a good versus bad life.

> Laura was living in an idealised future and unwilling to examine her past that she dismissed as irrelevant. By constantly looking to her external environment for the answer to life, Laura was missing the vital ingredient, which was to explore her own story, to admit her vulnerability, recognise that life was imperfect and to accept both her own and life's limitations. We both had to learn to sit with the un-known.

Whether we believe in God, in pink fairies or that there is nothing but bones or ashes after we die; all these beliefs have a sense of future time and what we are required to do before we die.

These four dimensions, similar to the leaves of the Wheel of Existence, are talked about separately so as to understand the concepts but are lived and experienced as parts of the whole person and their relationship to the world at large. Each of the worlds is linked and ideally held in a specific balance that is appropriate for each person in his or her personal setting and time of life. For instance, a Buddhist monk on retreat is likely to be more focused on his spiritual world, while an athlete preparing for a competition will concentrate on his physical dimension. The fourfold world makes it possible for clients and therapists to explore how clients exist on each dimension.

The exploration of the four worlds is also a powerful means for clients to delve into and challenge their value systems.

> Julian, for example, suffered panic attacks that he could describe in detail (the *Umwelt*), and which were related to his relationships in the *Mitwelt*. That is, he began not to want to go out and enjoy himself in case he had a panic attack in public. In his private, intimate world of the *Eigenwelt* he was suffering from a lack of self-confidence, while in his *Überwelt* he began to realise that he was scared of dying. In therapy, all four of these areas were considered as interrelated.

Listening to clients and understanding their relative position on these four dimensions can reveal where possible disparities lie. Some clients, for example, may be more preoccupied with one dimension to the virtual exclusion of another.

> John desired a perfect body and obsessively devoted time and energy to achieving this ideal. Nevertheless, he was aware that there was something 'wrong' in his obsessiveness. In therapy John began to realise that he had ignored all other aspects of his life, namely his spiritual, public, and to some extent his private world. He was now being challenged to reconsider his belief that his physical body and his desire for perfection was the only way to survive. John saw that what he was really doing was trying to escape rejection, which would normally throw him into despair. John is a good example of what can happen if the dimensions are dominated by one of the four worlds.

Although it is not necessary or even necessarily desirable to have an equal balance, if one of the four worlds dominates, exploration of the other three can open up whole new vistas of viewing one's experience of living. The four worlds, and how we express them, mirror our worldview and hence are another lens for understanding our being in the world.

11

Clarifying the Worldview

Man is made by his belief. As he believes, so he is.

Bhagavad Gita, 500 BCE

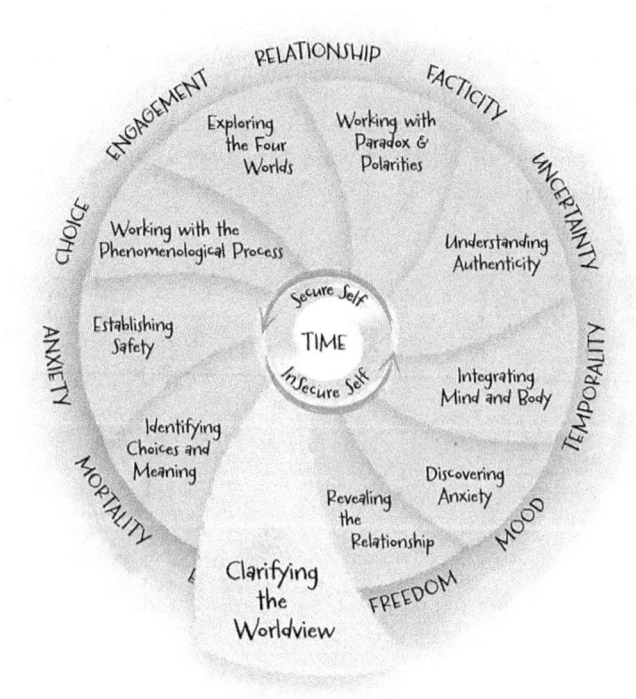

Source: Alison Strasser

Our worldview is our lens through which we understand and make sense of life. We create our worldview in responses to the ontological 'givens'. It includes our values, beliefs, assumptions and personal theories, and our perspectives on time, death, limitations, and possibilities, providing us with a structure and sense of 'certainty' that we greatly require within our uncertain world. This chapter focuses on exploring our worldview and examining how aspects of it become sedimented or stuck, limiting our choices and feasibly closing off our future potential.

In recent years, I have begun to name these embedded beliefs and values that comprise our worldview as 'personal principles', since, once established, they influence multiple facets of our lives. Generally, these personal principles emanate from our childhood interactions with others as we develop strategies to optimise our sense of personal safety.

> We return to Clara, whom we met in the previous chapter. Clara's mother would pit each of her four children against each other. Unwittingly, Clara learnt not to trust her siblings since they would ultimately attempt to undermine her achievements. As a child Clara believed that this competitive way of behaving would not only help her feel better about herself when she 'won' but was also as a means of winning affection and approval from her mother.
>
> These childhood experiences shaped Clara's ontic reactions to how she related to others. Superficially she was personable and could easily make friends but, in reality, she was continually on the alert for attacks by others. She would prepare for the 'attack' by bolstering herself through various strategies, such as always having a close friend who would advocate for her and would remain her buddy through thick and thin. This strategy appeared to both replicate and mitigate the way her siblings related to each other, which they did either as allies that couldn't falter or as betraying enemies.
>
> As an adult, Clara would tell great stories to her friends, creating conspiracy theories about her bosses. She also studied extensively, so that she was seen as an expert both in her field and in her understanding of human nature, thereby outsmarting any perceived competition. Invariably she would feel hurt when other people were chosen for particular tasks or friends would go out without inviting her. Even when discussing broader topics such as politics she would have to prove how clever she was and, therefore, somehow better than others. These behaviours were strategies to maintain her worldview that to be clever was to be liked and therefore a worthy person.

The creation of our worldview with its inherent principles is intrinsic to the existence of our being. The principles help us make meaning about our particular world. They reveal who we are, how we think and feel, and influence how we act towards others and ourselves (Spinelli, 2015). In this sense, we are our principles. For Clara, one of her personal principles was her ongoing experience of the world as competitive. Although contrary to her stated belief in the principle of equality and compassion, she acted as if others were competing with her; she was thus both defensive in her responses and on the alert to attack. This style of relating affected all her relationships (sexual, social, and work) because, sooner or later, she would experience the other person as being in competition with her and she would react accordingly.

People create a whole host of personal principles, a considerable percentage of which originate in cultural attitudes and which become imposed on us. These personal principles can be implied or explicitly manifested, permeate every aspect of our existence and often conflict with each other. They include modesty, exhibitionism, perfectionism, competence, calmness, bravery, compliance, loyalty, vulgarity, arrogance, pretension, naturalness, laziness, superiority, good judgement, cheating, deceit, tricking, risk taking, caution, competitiveness, independence, honesty, dishonesty. Values – such as loyalty, honesty, ambition, perfection, and material wellbeing – interact with our principles, benefiting, and helping us to be successful, to achieve goals and to maintain adept relations within society.

However, '[w]hat ultimately matters in existential work is to determine what it is that really matters to the clients, not what ought to matter to them' (van Deurzen, 2002, p. 106). In other words, in order for clients to move out of their childhood responses into the world of adult relationships, it can help to reflect on how they came to inherit their personal principles and their reasons for adopting them, and to understand both the benefits and limitations of them.

Clarifying the distinction between the principles and values that may have been imposed on us by others, and the principles and values that we truly cherish as our own, is a process that supports a way of becoming more authentic. Authenticity will be further explored in Chapter 15.

> Clara was battling with an inherent contradiction. Her father had always wanted her to take over the family law firm, reflecting the family belief that, as the eldest sibling, she would do so. Clara had indeed studied law at university, but, struggling to keep up, swore that she would never become a lawyer. Clara felt delighted and vindicated when she succeeded in getting a trainee job on a newspaper and, although her father expressed his pleasure, she also felt that she had disappointed him. His disillusionment niggled her but began to dissipate when she became a court reporter and was later appointed as the main legal writer. During therapy, Clara realised that she was still

> compromising herself in that it was the writing she enjoyed and not the intricacies and minutiae of the legal world.
>   In therapy Clara realised that she had been juggling her relationship with her father, keeping him at arm's length by neither entirely rebuffing him nor getting too close to him out of fear of his rejection of her. Clara had felt conflicted when she became a journalist and had moved into the legal area of journalism simply thinking she was keeping her father happy. Eventually she came to the conclusion that she was more interested in the world of theatre, even expressing the possibility of writing some of her own plays. Once Clara had teased out the values imposed on her by her parents and her own desires for herself, she succeeded, despite her ambivalence about how she thought her father might feel.

Sedimentation and the Strategies That We Employ to Sustain Them

When our personal principles are flexible, we are open to adapting to new circumstances, to hearing how others think and to expanding our own views. However, in our attempts to feel certainty, our values, beliefs or personal principles often become too fixed, too rigid or, in existential terms, 'sedimented'.

Sedimentation is an unusual word to apply in a therapeutic context. The term 'sediment' is normally used to describe 'the matter that settles at the bottom of a liquid' (Merriam Webster Dictionary, 2021). Essentially, existentially speaking, *sedimentation* refers to the way human beings settle into, or become stuck or fixed in certain beliefs and behaviour patterns (personal principles) that have deposited themselves deep down in our being-ness, in a similar fashion to the way sediment sinks to the bottom of a liquid. They become so enmeshed and intertwined with the way we behave in the everyday world that we are often totally unaware of their very existence. They are also very difficult or even impossible to unlearn.

> Peter spoke about when, at about the age of 3, he realised that he was different from others around him and he was terrified that his parents would discover this inherent defect. He described this revelation as an earthquake that shook up his entire life, his complete sense of being. Peter's only way to survive was to 'be nice' so as not to be disliked, to be compliant, to keep other people happy, by any means possible. He even talked about this way of understanding himself as a 'sediment' emanating from the original earthquake that

> was immoveable. As an adult, he always ensured that he remained invisible by creating a protective layer; he developed a stylishness, always immaculately groomed, his expensive shirts tailored to the last stitch. He believed that by these means nobody saw his true self. He believed that 'being nice' and looking perfect protected his parents from having to see, and be disappointed by, his 'badness'. His behaviours had become sedimented.

As clients begin to explore their underlying beliefs, it soon becomes apparent that their way of viewing their world is often quite rigid. Even when a belief is clearly wrong or not working, there is a determination to stick to their assumptions. This is not surprising, in that these assumptions and beliefs were usually adopted to provide the desired security but become more entrenched and increasingly sophisticated as the years pass. However, strategies and coping mechanisms useful in childhood may not always be entirely advantageous in adulthood, and therefore necessitate further exploration and reflection. A significant component of the therapist's task is to help the client not only to identify and understand their personal principles, but to examine how and in what ways they have become sedimented, and how they might simultaneously be both advantageous and damaging.

Clients often express surprise or even horror when discovering their own system of sedimentation; of how they fix or sediment their principle to maintain their position. Awareness is the first step towards shifting the sediment into a more flexible stance. Carla's sedimented belief was that life is competitive and she would automatically scan the horizon with the expectation that those around her would want to surpass her and she would be left feeling worthless. To arrive at a more flexible orientation, Carla would eventually find a different attitude or relationship to her understanding of the expression 'competitive'. She was able to see that not all people had the desire to overpower her and were not necessarily competitive themselves, but that some of her friends and work colleagues were, in fact, caring and had her interests at heart.

> However restricted, all sedimented beliefs serve to define the self construct and, as such, in most instances, the challenging of these beliefs is highly likely to be met with serious resistance because a challenge to any part of the self construct also challenges the whole of it. (Spinelli, 1994, p. 349)

Even a shift in our worldview can be experienced as a shift towards the uncertainties and anxieties that led to the creation, in the first place, of the sedimentation that has subsequently served us so well. It requires great commitment to shift our perspective.

> Adrian believed that his pessimism had helped him navigate the world as a Jewish child in post-war Germany. His mother was adamant that people were not to be trusted, advice that he took to heart, adding a personal angle that it was safest to be negative so that he could never be unduly surprised. He remembered a couple of incidents that he described as happiness or freedom: one was driving from home to his first job feeling a sense of freedom which he described effusively; the other was his viewing one of Van Gogh's sunflower paintings, the colours and movement of which he explained as having deeply touched him. We explored the possibilities and limitations of Adrian's pessimism and, although he intellectually understood the advantage of living with a more optimistic view, he left therapy when he realised that he was unable to shift away from this pessimistic stance. As an apparently powerful man who had built a business empire in the clothing business, he admitted to his cowardice. Yet Adrian was clear that it felt safer for him to stay with the sedimented certainty of the pessimism he knew than to walk into the territory of the unknown.

Conversely, a simple discernment can shift an old sedimented story.

> Max had spent most of his twenties in therapy to remove himself from his addictions and to understand why his father had not rescued him and his brother from their abusive stepmother. Surely his father, if he was a 'real' father, would have known that his stepmother beat him and berated him continuously for spoiling her relationship with his father? Now in his forties, in an 'aha' therapeutic moment, he realised that his father most probably had not known about the abuse. He had never told his father out of fear of further recrimination from his stepmother. Furthermore, his father would only have seen Max's attempts to placate his stepmother to avoid her wrath. Max had been a victim of his sedimentation that good fathers 'should know'. This revelation shifted the onus of responsibility from Max's father to himself and opened up pathways to reviewing all of his relationships.

We can be dogmatic or 'stuck' to such an extent that it is often hard to realise that there might be other ways of viewing the world or other ways of conducting our lives. We all have a vested interest in defending our old ways of thinking and our predictable, safe behaviours.

> Lynn's presenting problem was the difficulty she experienced in communicating with people, particularly in groups. During therapy Lynn became aware that one of her sedimentations was that of modesty; to 'show off' was perceived as a deadly sin to such an extent that the slightest manifestation of immodesty threw her into panic. As a result, she withdrew from any relationship in which there was a danger of being exposed.
>
> As the sessions progressed, Lynn realised that buried deep within her was a different kind of person, one that was extrovert and lively. She had vivid memories of a party when she was 5 years old, where she had joked, danced, and sung. She remembered how her joy was rudely interrupted when her mother dragged her from the room, screaming at her 'to stop showing off'. Lynn realised that her family, coming from a very restricted, religious Protestant background, condemned any kind of behaviour that could be regarded as flamboyant, judging it as rude and ill mannered.
>
> She could still feel the devastation of that experience and the worthlessness and aloneness she felt as she sat in her bedroom. Lynn remembers clearly how she soothed herself by angrily decrying that 'she would never give in to having such fun'. Although not overtly stated, Lynn had created a survival strategy to refrain from her gregarious, extroverted self that included withdrawing into a fantasy world where she found solace in literature and poetry. Indeed, she had maintained this pattern which revealed itself in her fear of communicating in groups. It was only when we spoke about this strategy that Lynn remembered saying to herself, at an early age, that she wouldn't allow herself to feel that devastated again.
>
> The driving force behind Lynn's sedimented beliefs was her inexorable longing for approval from her mother by remaining modest and unprepossessing. This sedimentation evolved into Lynn continually pressurising herself into pleasing people, refraining from 'showing off' by not talking about herself or even having an opinion. She became unable to express her ideas and lost confidence, feeling bad when she was rebuked and unable to achieve her goals – igniting a self-perpetuating cycle of loneliness, isolation, and poor self-esteem. On the other hand, her unassuming behaviour helped her to feel safe by 'not showing off'. Lynn was trapped in a 'Catch 22'.

The therapist challenged Lynn's 'showing off' episode at her parents' party to highlight her sedimentation that the only way to function effectively was to maintain her modesty. As a child Lynn had originally enjoyed the times that she had 'shown off', as it had attracted people's attention and she relished the freedom of dancing and singing. She had felt good about herself. However, her mother had so emphatically and repeatedly shown her disapproval that Lynn's value system had undergone a gradual reversal so that the positive elements of 'showing off' or having fun took on the negative connotation of self-importance and pretentiousness. She chose to remain unassuming, thus avoiding the disapproval and gaining the approval that she so cherished. Through these means Lynn's 'self-construct' became limited and contained, her saddest moment being when she admitted that even though she had done her utmost to please, she still felt her mother's disapproval.

In many ways, Lynn's sedimentation represents one of the many paths that we as human beings follow to search for approval and escape disapproval. The need for approval is so deeply ingrained in us that the form in which it manifests itself becomes prevalent in all avenues of life. Lynn's 'showing off' episode exemplified her need for approval from an audience to satisfy her self-esteem. On the other hand, her fear of disapproval manifested itself in her fear of public appearances. Lynn's issue was not her sedimented pattern of withdrawal and introversion, for in many ways this model was successful – she became a better student and gained an interest in literature and poetry that might not have occurred if she had remained an extrovert. Nor was her problem due to her sedimentation of gaining approval through her modesty, or her fear of disapproval by 'showing off'. Her true issue was slightly further entrenched in that it stemmed from her fear of criticism, which was synonymous with the feelings of rejection she experienced when publicly criticised by her mother. Rejection became synonymous with loneliness, being an outsider, and unable to join in because of her lack of self-esteem. To avoid these devastating feelings, at an early age Lynn began her lifelong quest to gain approval, avoid disapproval, and hence maintain her sense of self-esteem.

Although rigid sedimentations may appear to have started in childhood, there are also others, which may seem to have been created in adulthood. In fact, there is no need to search for the so-called sources of sedimentations, as there is always a multitude of events that create, recreate, and reinforce those sedimented perceptions.

In therapy, once clients can come to terms with the idea of sedimentation, they can challenge their entrenched beliefs and behaviour systems. Some insights and a change of perception may ensue, as exemplified by Lynn. In therapy she was able to question whether her modesty always served her positively, and, conversely, whether showing off always affected her negatively. This challenge set in motion a chain reaction, in which she rapidly began to realise that she possessed the power to choose her alternative behavioural options.

Our need to retain our sedimentation is also caught up in our perceived notion of self, our identity. When we realise that our only exit from our current 'stuckness' is to review and shift our essential value and belief system, it can feel like a metaphorical death of self. We might fear taking on those values and behaviours we have tried for many years not to. Adrian feared that, in freedom, he would no longer have the sharp 'edginess' on life that kept him on the alert; Carla, once she realised that she was competitive, saw this aspect of her identity as crucial for success; Lynn had taken up a humble, modest stance as a 5-year-old, from which time she had become accustomed to remaining in the background, a position that had served her well by keeping her at arm's length, protecting her from other people's criticism.

There are an infinite number of possible values that we will latch onto at some point in our lives. Indeed, these values dictate everyday encounters with people and the decisions made during our life, both helpful and harmful. Often it is not until the start of therapy that clients will begin to realise how strict a grip their underlying values have over them and the courage it takes to begin to extricate themselves from the destructive safety of their sedimentations.

As Paul Tillich, the Christian German-American, existential philosopher and theologian said, 'The courage to be is rooted in the God who appears when God disappears in the anxiety of doubt' (1980).

The Therapist's Worldview

The structure of the Wheel of Existence and its graphical representation also serve as a format for therapists to understand their own personal worldview and its ramifications, both positive and negative. This is important when attempting to tolerate, understand and resonate with clients' issues and their worldviews and when reflecting on what is occurring within the relational space with one's clients and supervisees. When thinking about working with worldview in therapy, as therapists we can assume that many of our clients' issues will in some way resonate with our own. Indeed, this is the starting point for entering into and understanding a client's worldview. As therapists, if we too can become aware of and process our own issues, we are more likely to be able to identify with a client's problems and pain. This attunement helps us both enquire of our client's worldview with more caring and allows us to identify and challenge contradictions or discrepancies as they emerge. Known variously as empathy, presence, attunement or resonance, it is also described as relational depth, where 'the therapist is attuned to the client's physicality and emotions as they are with the client's thoughts' (Cooper & Mearns, 2005, p. 40). The therapist's openness to reflecting on her own worldview enables this phenomenological work. Values, beliefs, and personal principles will inevitably interpose into the relationship with the client.

A story of a supervisee serves as an illustration of how a client's problem can strike at the heart of the therapist's issues.

> Matthew worked in a prison and, in a supervision session, related his dilemma with a particular inmate. His client was profuse in 'vividly' describing how he had stabbed his girlfriend yet was convinced that it wasn't him that had dug the knife into her back. He adamantly maintained that 'it was as if I wasn't there', but would reveal his anger, anxiety, and violent emotions as he talked about the physical act of the knife penetrating and exiting his girlfriend's torso, leaving Matthew feeling dismayed and confounded. As Matthew relived this exchange in his supervision, he became aware of his own anxiety, realising that he also carried within himself a seed of aggression, and that sometimes it is only a tiny distinction, a hair's breadth, that differentiates us from each other. By identifying and exploring his own reaction Matthew was able to shift from dismay and incomprehension to a more empathic position, which helped him to both resonate with his client and to also identify and challenge the discrepancies.

In this example, the therapist was not initially aware of the similarity of his emotional response to that of his client. All too often, the therapist will hear clients speak of personal principles that appear similar to their own, yet there will be different stories and emotional connections. These need to be carefully listened to; if not, there is a danger of responding to one's own story and not the client's.

The idea of independence is an old and well-established personal principle of mine that I cultivated as the eldest child of three daughters. Independence is a complex phenomenon in that it gives me a sense of freedom not to be tied down, and yet I often feel ungrounded and insecure when I am not in a regime and routine with other people.

> Veronica, a client, was also the eldest child and was fiercely independent to the point that she was reduced to bartering for shoes, rather than ask for financial assistance from her ex-husband. She believed that now that they were separated, she had no rights and had to take care of herself. It was easy for me to connect with her overwhelming confusion and ungroundedness when talking about the possibility of asking for something for herself. I too didn't like to ask for help because of my pride and my desire to show my parents that I could do things my way. However, in reality, had I asked for help, it would have been lovingly and unconditionally offered; in Veronica's world, help from her parents would have had unbearable consequences. To help her, I needed to understand that her story was different from mine and had to bracket my own.

Understanding and clarifying a client's worldview is seemingly simple yet also complex. To preserve our personal principles, we will create behaviours and adopt coping strategies often convoluted and bizarre to ensure that we maintain the identity that we have created. The moment we form a specific self-belief, the opposite is also true, as the next chapter will show. As with Veronica and myself, independence was the necessary survival position to feel optimistic and hopeful, but the polarity of dependence that generated feelings of despair had been ignored. Our stories and strategies were very different, but we could connect in our shared vulnerable space. The journey is to unpack the hidden gems that hide within the folds of our sedimented polarities.

12

Working with Paradox and Polarities

If I had a world of my own, everything would be nonsense. Nothing would be what it is because everything would be what it isn't. And contrariwise, what it is, it wouldn't be, and what it wouldn't be, it would.

　　　　　　　　　　　　　　Lewis Carroll, *Alice's Adventures in Wonderland*

Source: Alison Strasser

Time-Limited Existential Therapy: The Wheel of Existence, Second Edition. Alison Strasser.
© 2022 John Wiley & Sons Ltd. Published 2022 by John Wiley & Sons Ltd.

Living with Paradox

Existentialism, almost by definition, is a philosophy of ambiguity and the absurd. Kierkegaard postulated that human experiences are underpinned by paradox. 'What a man knows he cannot seek, since he knows it; and what he does not know he cannot seek, since he does not even know for what to seek' (1967, p. 9). As humans, we are constantly reaching out, attempting to find a grain of truth, a semblance of certainty, only to realise that, once again, truth and certainty have eluded us.

There are many definitions for the word 'paradox', but the broad dictionary consensus is that it is 'a statement that seems to contradict itself but may nonetheless be true' (The Free Dictionary, 2021). Similarly, in existential terms, paradox is usually talked about as a position that we find ourselves in that is contradictory, ambiguous, and simultaneously true. As such, on the surface it is almost by definition never fully resolvable.

In the ontological realm, we 'know' the hum of meaninglessness, yet in the ontic realm we are constantly navigating the tension of meaning and meaninglessness. Paradoxically, meaning is not a solid structure to acquire but a construct that continually shifts and is therefore beyond one's reach. Even as we contemplate meaning, the meaning changes. 'The courageous living within this dilemma . . . is the source of human creativity' (May, 1967, p. 20).

So too, as we reflect on our personal worldview, inconsistencies or paradoxes arise in our principles, values, and beliefs. Spinelli (2015) describes these as 'tensions in existence polarities', which he extrapolated from Wahl's (2003) work on existential tensions, in which Wahl argues that a sense of incompleteness or an inability to fully resolve our experience of living in this world is constant.

These tensions relate to our personal principles, as discussed in Chapter 11, and come to the fore when we reflect on our personal version of the polarity of these principles. A child finds it hard to understand that one can love and hate at the same time. Yet, this is often one of the first tensions that we learn to navigate as we enter into more adult relationships. At the personal, sedimented level, these principles are harder to manoeuvre because they are tied to our sense of identity and perception of safety.

> For instance, Clara, whom we've met earlier, could not contemplate holding both the idea of competitiveness and equality, so it was easier to privilege equality and disown her competitiveness. Even when she became aware of her own competitiveness it was hard for her to accept that this was as much

> part of her as was her desire for equality and caring. Over time, and as Clara explored the pros and cons of both positions, she began to enjoy the benefits of being competitive and even laughed at herself when she caught herself manipulating others to advance her position. She showed her courage by pushing herself to try different ways of approaching situations and then reflecting on the outcome both for herself and others.

It is often the case that in choosing one position, the opposite, or its polarity, is also true. For example, if independence connotes a positive value for someone, dependence may well suggest a negative meaning and will be linked to their personal stories that corroborate this polar position. From the age of 5, Lynn (whom we met in Chapter 11) had lived with and by her value of modesty in an attempt to retain a good relationship with her mother, and Clara had internalised the competitive value her mother had orchestrated as the only way to live in a dangerous world. For Lynn, the opposite of modesty was showing off, and for Clara, the competitiveness by which she lived masked her fear of its opposite, loss.

> What stands out as a basic principle is that human existence is a struggle between opposites. There are two sides to every experience. Each argument has a counter argument. Positive aspects turn out to have negative counterparts and vice versa. People always find themselves somewhere on the continuum between life and death, good and bad, positive and negative, active and passive, happiness and sadness, closeness and distance. (van Deurzen, 2012, p. 65)

Polarities

Though the list is endless, Table 12.1 identifies some examples of values and their polarities. Clients often choose to live at one end of the spectrum, and by doing so may attempt to ignore the existence of their polarity. Lynn avoided people that were gregarious, seeing them as 'show-offs', and Clara would denigrate her work colleagues as competitive vipers.

Such denial leads to a belief that the polarity of their personal principle is not part of their worldview. As therapy progresses, the polarities become less fixed and the client begins to appreciate both the benefits of the ignored polarity and the detrimental impact of its disavowal. Sometimes, exploring the positive features of a client's disavowed or 'negative principle' facilitates significant awareness. Since all values are entrenched in our personal history, their meaning and their polarity will be subjective.

Table 12.1 Values and their polarities

Positive value	Negative value
Modesty	Showing off
Competition	Equality
Dependence	Independence
Monogamy	Promiscuity
Strong	Weak
Fair	Unjust
Right	Wrong
Tranquillity	Anxiety
Loyalty	Disloyalty
Refinement	Vulgarity
Security	Insecurity
Slim	Fat
Order	Chaos
Peace of mind	Agitation
Knowing all	Ignorance
Honesty	Cheating
Natural	Contrived
Intellectual	Intuitive
Superior	Inferior
Good judgement	Bad judgement
Kind	Selfish
Make others feel good	Make others feel bad
To please others	To please oneself

Source: Freddie & Alison Strasser (Strasser & Strasser, 1997)

Ian found that he had a problem in asking questions. He realised that as a young boy he had been known to possess an extraordinary mental capacity for remembering information. His father enjoyed showing Ian off to his friends and would make Ian 'perform' by asking him questions. One day, he failed to give the right answer to the question, 'What is the capital of Borneo?' He was so shocked by his father's reprimand that he became seriously depressed. As a result of this and other reinforcing events, he gradually developed a belief about himself – an ontic response to his father's rebuke – as someone who had the duty to know everything, that being knowledgeable was desirable and that, as a knowledgeable person, he felt affirmed and validated. Conversely, if he was not knowledgeable, he was obviously 'good for nothing' and dislikeable. Each time he was unable to answer a question, therefore, he would feel utterly invalidated. Over time he developed the habit of refraining from asking questions because he did not want to reveal his ignorance. When he really wanted to know something, he automatically made a statement of fact, pushing the other person into an argument. Through this elaborate method Ian would often discover the answer to his question. This way of interacting had become so ingrained that Ian was totally unaware of his convoluted way of both gaining information and keeping himself from feeling worthless.

As Ian became aware of his sedimentation and his personal strategy of avoiding questions so that he did not have to feel incompetent and desolate, he began to explore possible alternatives. He wondered whether there were other ways to be validated instead of being unreservedly knowledgeable. The most important question he posed was: 'Do I really have to know everything to be accepted by others, and is this really possible?' Thus, he was able to adopt a system that was less rigid and that took into account his polarity, ignorance, with a more authentic and softer attitude. He realised that his belief in his ignorance was the version, his sedimentation, he had assumed as a child in reaction to his father's persistent questions. Moreover, he was surprised to recognise that he was harder on himself than on others, for he did not expect others to have such a universal and complete knowledge. Slowly he began to see that his belief in his state of ignorance could offer alternative views such as 'willing to know' or 'discussions can be fun'. Additionally, he grasped that his strategy of pretending to know everything was a form of self-sabotage, because his intention of being liked and valued often failed as he was often viewed as arrogant and pretentious.

Until we begin to explore our underlying value system, often through a conduit offered by the values of which we are more aware, we cannot begin to understand the intricate patterns of thinking, feeling, behaving, and relating that ensue. As we work with polarities or apparent contradictions, a new kind of 'and' emerges that is inclusive of both ends of the spectrum and imbued with different 'flavours'. What begins as a personal paradox, as a personal fixed sedimentation, can mutate into a more fluid, flexible principle, allowing more options for alternative choices to be made.

Dissociation

A value's opposite, its polarity, is masked within the sedimentation of our belief system. Sometimes this opposite value is infused with so intense a feeling of vulnerability, powerlessness or being out of control that it has had to be banished out of existence. In existential therapy, this phenomenon is called dissociation and most existential therapists talk about these dissociated aspects as being 'out of awareness' or as unreflected states of being. A person who believes they are independent, for example, may be unaware of the demands they put on others because recognition of these demands would nullify or challenge their belief about their independence and necessitate their acknowledgement of their dependent behaviours.

'The question of dissociation revolves around an individual's self-concept in that it supposes a dissonance between beliefs about one's self and the experience of one's self' (Spinelli, 1994, p. 222). It is almost as if there are degrees of sedimentation: the deeper the sedimentation, the more likely it is that the polarity, the opposite position that we ascribe to, is dissociated. However, while out of the individual's awareness, it may be patently obvious to others. For instance, when my therapist pointed out that my expectations of others related to my neediness, I reacted in horror. It took me a while for me to be able to recognise a truth about myself.

Clients will often come to therapy because they are aware of repeated patterns of feelings and behaviours, but the sedimentation and its dissociation that underpin those behaviours may come as a complete surprise. Clara, who valued the principle of equality and believed that she behaved accordingly, initially was not receptive to the idea that others saw her as competitive.

> After the death of her parents, Janice's siblings decided to sell the family home, without her consent. As a result, Janice felt very isolated and depressed. Realising that she needed help to overcome her depression, Janice began therapy with the wish to find a 'real' relationship with someone who was 'straight and honest' and in whom she could trust. Until a friend put her arms around her and she shrank away in horror, she had not realised how much she abhorred any physical contact. In spite of wanting to surround herself with trustworthy people, she had not understood how her recoiling behaviour decreased her chances of finding such friends. Janice's feelings had become dissociated from her behaviour, with the result that she was both unable to accept any emotional closeness and unaware that she was repelling the very contact she had thought she wanted.
>
> Initially, Janice blamed herself and her anger outbursts for keeping others away. As we talked, she recognised that her inherent dislike of getting close to

> anyone physically was part of an old belief system. In therapy, she traced her stance back to when she was a young girl and hated being in close proximity to her violent father, especially after he had been drinking. This fear of proximity was exacerbated following the sexual assault by her uncle when she was 17, the one male in her family that she could talk to and thought she could trust. She entered the Church as a novice nun at 22, as an escape from having to come to terms with her fear. She expected it to be a safe and honest place, but unfortunately this hope was not fulfilled long term, as after a disagreement with her Mother Superior 10 years later, Janice was told she was not suitable to be a nun and was cast out. She continued to live an isolated existence until her parents died.
>
> One of her strongest personal principles was the value of being 'straight and honest', for both herself and others. Janice wanted to trust, yet her experience belied this wish. She firmly believed that one of her strengths was that she 'spoke her mind' and that she was always honest, even if it got her into trouble with friends and those in authority. It became clear that her polarity was the belief that people were devious – or in a child's language, liars – which linked back to her experiences with her father and her uncle whom she learnt not to trust.
>
> Her life-long maxim that she was open and honest became fixed as part of her identity, giving her a sense of righteousness and self-belief. It was hard for her to challenge this and to recognise that that she was unable to express her likes and dislikes and that her ritual of remaining silent was inconsistent with her principle of being open and honest. It took being violently attacked by her brother, years later, for Janice to finally recognise that her silence had contributed to this event. It would still be a long road for Janice to learn to trust but she emerged from her silence, telling her sister about her ex-husband's abuse of her and then moving to a new house so as to be in closer proximity to her sister.

Therapy helps clients expand their awareness of the advantages and the restrictions of their sedimented position as well as how its polarity may have been banished or dissociated. As clients enlarge their story, they are also broadening their belief and value systems and thus are more able to see the same situation from different perspectives.

> Once Clara saw that she approached life through a lens of competition, and had a pervasive drive to win, she was also able to accept how vulnerable she was to its polarity, her fear of losing out to others. Significantly, at the point of

> this realisation, she disappeared from therapy, giving excuses about demands of work. On her return, Clara admitted that she had spiralled into the depths of despair as she couldn't accept herself as 'second best', an image evoked through our conversation about who she might be if she wasn't 'a winner'. She realised that her fear of losing was equivalent to feeling like a failed person. Paradoxically, when she reviewed her life, she saw that by fearing defeat she had missed out on the potential gains that losing might bring. Finally, she wryly admitted that in her eagerness to always win, she had not seen that the victory could have been perceived as a loss, and vice versa. Her understanding of competition was becoming less polarised and more fluid.
>
> In therapy, an awareness of dissociated feelings from the actual behaviour can cause overwhelming emotions for our clients. However, Clara did not concede to this mood for long and instead pulled herself into action. She began to appreciate that seeing the world as competitive was sometimes healthy, giving her advantages that she could now specifically name, while acknowledging that losing did not always have a negative an outcome, nor was it something to be feared. Conversely, she did not have to be afraid of not succeeding.

It is heart-warming to see clients embrace therapy and to observe their shifts.

> When Janice left therapy, she could talk about her anger, she could laugh about her 'slyness' and she could cry about her parents. She had begun to see that her silence had protected her as a child and adolescent but that silence in her adulthood had left her vulnerable and open to further abuse. She was beginning to take more responsibility and to be more authentically 'open and honest'.
>
> Finally, Janice's story also provides us with an example of how our worldview and the dynamics of sedimentation and dissociation might overlap with the issue of time. Janice began therapy pleased that it was limited to 12 sessions, and relieved, she later realised, to hear that she was 'not that bad', that she could treat the sessions in a transient manner and thus also avoid the discomfort of feeling too close. During the tenth session, however, when I reminded her that there were only two sessions remaining, Janice accused me of abandoning her and stormed out of the room. The following week, she apologised. This event gave us the opportunity to explore how she felt about finishing and how she had experienced my reminder as a lie, as a means to get rid of her. Ironically, it was in the moment of my 'honest' acknowledgement of

> our ending that she felt abandoned and reacted in the only way she knew, through anger.
> Janice realised during this last session that she did not want to finish therapy, after all, and still wanted to work on her anger and her distrust. We agreed to continue on an open-ended basis. Janice's feelings of abandonment and rejection would emerge at every break. She would demurely accept my departures but would voice her anger on my return. Over the following three years of therapy, Janice finally accepted that my holiday breaks were not a personal vendetta to dispose of her presence, which she'd felt when banished from the convent. In point of fact, my comings and goings eventuated in Janice coyly admitting that she knew that she was in my thoughts even in my absence. Janice had broadened her narrative, giving her more choice and additional emotional responses to events that had previously triggered her anger. In this respect, she had gained more flexibility around her principle of honesty and dishonesty and broadened her values and sense of self to embrace her formerly dissociated feelings.

Lynn integrated her showing off so that it became less of a highly charged stigma; Clara took up the battle and acknowledged that competition was part of life and sought out cooperative board games to play with friends. Ian included his ignorant side in his conversations and was enjoying how he could learn from others without feeling a fool; while Janice was observing her anger and using it to detect how she was feeling about situations and people that she didn't trust.

Lynn's 'showing off', Clara's competitiveness, Ian's argumentativeness and Janice's reticence are all examples of chosen personal principles that were locked or sedimented in earlier lives for self-protection – as were their valued polarities: modesty (Lynn), being a 'winner' (Clara), competence (Ian) and openness and honesty (Janice). Therapy helped to uncover how these personal principles inhibited the desired hopes and dreams of each of these individuals, as is the case for us all. Through exploration, they began to unlock their sedimentations and explore opposites and options. In reality, as adults, we have the capacity to view and review our past choices and, in the process, we may realise that the meanings we attached to these earlier events have also changed, opening us up to new possibilities and new choices.

13

Identifying Choices and Meaning

The very meaninglessness of life forces man to create his own meaning.
Stanley Kubrick, *Stanley Kubrick Interviews* (2001)

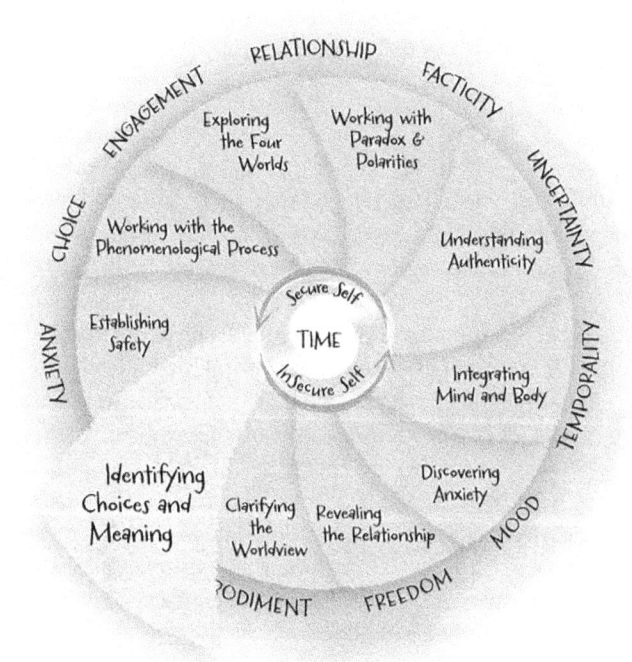

Source: Alison Strasser

Meaning

One of the common themes in existential philosophy is that our being-in-the-world, our living, is without an intrinsic meaning.

For Sartre, nothingness (no-thing-ness) is at the heart of human existence:

> What do we mean by saying that existence precedes essence? We mean that man first of all exists, encounters himself, surges up in the world – and defines himself afterwards. If man, as the existentialist sees him, is not definable, it is because to begin with he is nothing. He will not be anything until later, and then he will be what he makes of himself. (1973, p. 28).

Each of us experiences at least moments – and even long periods – when life appears pointless and meaningless. Sartre (1958) and Camus (1942) believe that the world, and indeed life itself, is without intrinsic meaning, that it appears meaningless. Sartre (1958) writes about the anguish that arises from the 'nothingness' that is constantly a part of us. 'We can never achieve the solidity and certainty of an object like a tree but must instead live with the anguish of knowing we are a "no-thing", needing to make choices about who or what we care to become' (Langdridge, 2013, p. 82). There is no constant self since, in our choosing, we are also creating and shifting our sense of who we believe we are. In Sartrean terms, we create meaning and this shifting sense of self out of the ashes of nothing.

A meaningful life does not appear by magic but is a purposeful process of choices that we make on our path towards becoming, towards a more authentic being. Heidegger's (1962) position is philosophically nuanced in that he explains that we are thrown into the world that is already imbued with meaning. We find ourselves in a world, and in a world that matters to us in that we are attached to the various outcomes of our choices. Our life 'task' is to incessantly choose our responses to all that life 'throws up', including our innate knowledge of our finitude and ultimate temporary existence.

Heidegger (1962) considers that we are 'thrown' into the world that is defined by place, timing, and our specific culture; that the world we are born into has already been imbued with meaning and routines created by others. As we move into this 'thrown' world, we choose the meanings and structures that make sense or give us feelings of certainty.

Essentially, this particular existential stance takes the position that the onus is on humans to make meaning for themselves and not to place this responsibility on God, parents or even beliefs that are not of our own choosing. The inherent paradox is that humans require a whole array of meanings to make sense of the how we live and the 'why' of existence.

Viktor Frankl, the Austrian neurologist and psychiatrist, having suffered a dire existence from 1942 to 1945 in Theresienstadt, Kaufering, Turckheim, and Auschwitz, where he lost most members of his immediate family, survived the atrocities of those concentration and death camps. Frankl maintained that it was the meaning that he found within his torturous experiences that helped him to survive the horrors of the Holocaust. He found, amongst his fellow inmates, that those who could assemble some kind of self-meaning, whether in the form of spirituality or the wish to survive to relate their stories, had more chance of surviving than those who could not find meaning. Inmates without a meaning literally lost the will to live. He devoted his remaining years 'to helping others find their meaning' (1963). This exploration of the 'search for meaning' became the foundation for 'logotherapy', the therapeutic approach that Frankl developed and which has survived beyond his death in at the age of 92.

Most people struggle with how to live within an acceptable equilibrium between the poles of meaning and a life without inherent meaning. It's difficult for us to endure the anxieties that erupt in the face of this paradox. On the one hand, the existential position is that there is no inherent meaning, and, on the other, that we require meaning to live a meaningful existence. A crisis of meaning may equate to a sense of meaninglessness and is inclusive of a whole array of classified symptoms such as depression, anxiety, addictions, and lack of identity.

Depression, as viewed from this perspective, is connected to a person's lack of meaningful existence. Sometimes this mood is transitory, in that something has happened such as loss of a job, death of a partner or moving to a different location. These changes throw up the existential themes of loneliness, despair, and questions around meaning and what no longer makes sense. Most of us will have periods where we feel as if life has lost its purpose and there is an aimless sense of a world of nothingness. Emmy van Deurzen aptly writes about 'a crisis of meaning' (van Deurzen, 2012) as a significant reason for clients starting therapy.

Often when clients are in the depth of their depression or despair they develop a belief in something, whether in some sort of spirituality, transcendence or a trust in themselves or others. Out of bleak nothingness, they begin to re-establish a meaningfulness to their lives. Therapy helps in that it can free them from their old, sedimented, highly limiting meaning systems and move forward with a new meaning. At a fundamental level, this is what the existentialists mean by choice. Here, for numerous reasons, the client chooses to take a different position, to refocus their meaning that will bring about change(s) in their life. '[Clients] may find themselves able to create new meaning where life had become apathetic and listless. They may be delighted to reveal a new depth to themselves and their lives that leads to passionate rather than depressed living. They may recover their own spirit of adventure and faith in themselves and the world around them' (van Deurzen, 2012, p. 237).

> Marianne described herself as depressed. A significant part of her therapy was dedicated to exploring the link between her depression and meaninglessness. She also suffered from insomnia and at times was so greatly incapacitated that she was unable to work. She was in a high-powered job and had a good reputation within her profession. Marianne attributed her depression to her continuing and relentless squabbles with her superiors in the office. However, as Marianne began to shift the focus of her exploration in therapy from her business to her private life, she became aware that it was the nature of her relationship with her partner that possibly accounted for her lack of meaning and purpose rather than the situation at work. As the 'second woman' to her partner, who was a married man with children, it began to dawn on her that her sense of meaninglessness was directly related to her choice of relationship which was preventing her from having the closer and more meaningful relationship she desired and to have the children that she had always expected to have.
>
> Although therapy helped her understand the link between her depression and her choice of relationship, she was unable to remove herself from the situation. Her greater awareness did not alter her sense of hopelessness since she now felt more of a failure with no one to blame but herself. She needed to find the courage to make changes and to trust in something different.
>
> In relationships, Marianne had metaphorically lost her voice, seemingly succumbing to others, yet inwardly seething and feeling as if she was powerless and had no choice. She would initially blame others for undermining her voice, until she acknowledged her own contribution in not speaking out and admitting her wants and needs. In therapy, as she began to challenge her own patterns and beliefs, Marianne developed greater faith in herself and in understanding that her desire to be loved by her partner was not burdensome or demanding. Before the conclusion of her 12-week therapy she was more assertive with her partner, clarifying what she wanted from the relationship. In her last session, she announced that she was pregnant.
>
> A year later, Marianne rang for an appointment, wishing to introduce her son. Her life had turned around when she chose to prioritise her relationship with her partner and, now, her son over her working life. Simultaneously, her working life became less important and the disputes that she had with her superiors took on less significance. As Marianne became aware of how her lack of voice had left her angry and lost, she could now make different choices.

The French existentialists, such as Sartre (1958) and Camus (1984), write about life as absurd and how our challenge as humans is to navigate our way through the maze of life's incongruities or paradoxes. The irrationality that 'surrounds man until his ultimate end' is in direct contrast to the way humans long for clarity and meaning (Camus, 1984). That humans cannot accept life without meaning, and yet there is no clearly prescribed meaning, is one of the numerous paradoxes of existence.

In line with notions of absurdity and the belief that meaning is not derived from God but is personal and not prescribed, the French existentialists described themselves as atheists. However, this viewpoint is only one perspective and writers such as Kierkegaard (1989), Tillich (1980), and Frankl (1963) emphasised the notion that spirituality and meaning are *sine qua non* and a necessary condition for living well.

> Jonathan described himself as depressed and, before commencing therapy, sent through a series of poems that he felt portrayed his current state of mind. Raised by adoptive parents in Canada, who were highly academic, he discovered at 18 that his birth parents were poor and uneducated, and it was hard for him to reconcile these two divergent histories. He had gone to university with expectations of graduating as a lawyer but instead disappeared down the path of rock and roll, often ending his nights in an alcoholic stupor or drug-related come-down.
>
> As an adoptee, he would describe his terror of abandonment and his intense feeling of never belonging. At the ontological level, he had been metaphorically thrown out of his birth mother to arrive in his adopted family. His ontic reaction was to adopt a belief that he had been deposited on Earth by extra-terrestrials and was now living an entirely foreign culture. This belief helped Jonathan come to terms with his sense of difference but still left him floundering about how to be accepted, especially when he now had four parents to please.
>
> At the age of 28 he met an Australian, married, emigrated to Sydney and within 2 years was divorced. Jonathan was floundering. He didn't want to return to Canada, he was lonely in Sydney, and he felt obliged to stay in contact with both sets of parents. The only place he felt safe was in his job which was routine and unexciting.
>
> In a nutshell, Jonathan felt abandoned by both sets of parents, his ex-wife and ultimately himself. During therapy, he came to realise that he had always blamed his birth mother and adopted parents for making him so miserable, accusing his mother for not being brave enough to keep him and his adopted parents for expecting him to be like them. It was easier to blame others than own up to his circumstances.
>
> As Jonathan came to understand how he was being defined by what he thought others wanted of him, it dawned on him that he had chosen to be

> what he believed others expected of him. He had little sense of what he wanted for himself or what would give him meaning. Now it was time to choose to live differently, to find what he wanted for himself.
> As he reflected on this, it dawned on him that he had inadvertently stumbled into a career as a librarian that was non-threatening and indeed amply interesting. As Jonathan came to accept that he didn't need to be a megastar or even strive for promotion, he started going out with work colleagues, made new friends and ultimately remarried and began his own family. Jonathan's meaning emerged as he began to pay less attention to other people's expectations and appreciated that he was happy within his world of books, films and creating online environments.

We are constantly striving to make meaning against the backdrop of meaninglessness and uncertainty. Our ontic responses may help or hinder us in this pursuit. We can always throw out our *thrown-ness*, as both Marianne and Jonathan came to be able to do, and find new modes of living, personal ways to create meaning. When meaning can be created within our awareness of the ontological givens that life is without inherent meaning and is underpinned by doubt and uncertainty, we are more likely to be able to live authentically, in good faith.

Choice and Freedom

> *Between stimulus and response there is a space. In that space is our power to choose our response. In our response lies our growth and our freedom.*
> Viktor Frankl, *Man's Search for Meaning* (1963)

Choice and freedom are complex phenomena. Many people are attracted to the prospect of freedom but, in his assertion that we are 'condemned' to be free, Sartre (1958) reminds us that freedom can be experienced almost as a curse. Sartre argued that, as life is without inherent meaning, devoid of universal values, ethics or religion, we, as individuals, are required to take complete responsibility for our actions. This position deprives us of the illusion that guidance can legitimately be sought, and blame legitimately apportioned externally. At the same time, it offers us countless opportunities to make choices, including the opportunity to choose to create meaning in our lives. Every action – or indeed, inaction – it has been argued, involves making a choice. Whether we choose or do not choose, as the latter involves the choice not to choose, we are always exercising choice.

However, in deeply engaging with the complex implications of choice, humans may find themselves face to face with uncertainty. In an attempt to resolve this uncomfortable state, we may question ourselves over our actions and our interpretations, try to second-guess our motives or the motives of others, ruminate over several ways of understanding the same situation, including all the alternative opinions that other people hold. However, all interpretations are fluid and have no inherent objective truth. When we realise that our interpretations are only our subjective truth and become attentive to our temporality, we recognise that we are mortal and will potentially die without completing all our desires – a realisation which often precipitates an overall lack of meaning and purpose.

The philosopher Merleau-Ponty (1962) believes that we are mostly unaware of the choices we are making and, unlike Sartre, he asserts that we thus do not always actively choose. He argues that 'freedom is only gained in the way we act. In my actions I show and create my significance and that of others and the world as well' (van Deurzen, 2010, p. 97). This links neatly to the concept of sedimentations discussed previously, in which we choose to act or live in a particular way as a reaction to past circumstances. We may not be actively aware of these choices, yet they drive us in particular directions. It is only when we actively reflect on these choices and respond with open awareness that we are acting in our freedom.

It is not uncommon for clients to feel that they are stuck, believing that they have only limited – or no – options available. For example, given that the facts (our facticity) that we are born tall or short, that we are children of single parents or that we come from a large family, are born English or Indian, are immutable, it may well seem that choice is non-existent. Despite this perception, at the very least we have different ways of viewing the situation we find ourselves in. We may not be able to change our circumstances, but we can choose our attitude, our ontic response. With such an understanding of choice, an infinite number of possibilities to exercise one's freedom to choose become available to us.

The existential position contends that we choose to create ourselves and that there are always many possibilities available from which to choose. These possibilities, and indeed our freedom, need to be discovered *within* our limitations and, often, against the backdrop of a sense of meaninglessness. The sections of the Wheel, which deal with our ontic responses, include such human limitations. To deny, avoid or ignore the limitations inherent in our lives is to deny or avoid the opportunity for authenticity and, thus, to live in what Sartre deemed to be 'bad faith'. Since existentialism involves the notion of people's freedom, it also points to our ability to choose our response, our interpretation of events and how to create meaning from our surrounding environment. In other words, we can 'throw off our thrown condition in a movement where it seizes hold of its possibilities, where it acts in a concrete situation' (Critchley, 2009) and choose different interpretations.

Often the naive questions offered by the therapist commence a process whereby clients can look at the same situation from a different perspective. Therapy gives

Identifying Choices and Meaning | 139

permission to the client to explore and find alternative narratives or explanations to the concrete past or the facts about life that they cannot change. Discovering or acknowledging meaning can alter our worldview and indeed our direction in life. Meaning need not be attached to some 'positive' moral value. It can be derived from – take – many forms; it can be attached to material economic progress, to behaviours and practices such as working at an achievement or to creative pursuits such as writing or painting, to name but a few.

Each of the sections of the Wheel also provides a way of understanding the various elements of how we navigate the vagaries of existence and can help us ponder the questions of how to be human. As we follow this path, the choices, within the limitations, become more apparent. It certainly appears, though, that to find our own path we have to confront, and bear, the demons of meaninglessness and take it upon ourselves to find or rediscover the values that are worthy of our existence

Often, this path takes us to the realisation that different choices need to be made – or at a minimum, a change in perspective.

> Jonathan realised that his path to freedom was to choose to stop responding to others' expectations and to find and act on his own choices. He also shifted his old narrative to encompass the novel idea that his birth mother had given him up for adoption hoping for a better life for him. Furthermore, Jonathan realised that his adopted parents might be demanding but they gave him an education and a view of the world that many people would be envious of.

> Clara blamed her mother for everything that was going wrong in her life. As therapy progressed, she began to realise that her mother had come from a position of caring rather than judgement. She developed a greater understanding that her mother's life had been hard and that she had wanted greater security for Clara and her siblings through education and financial advantage. She became kinder towards her mother. As she exercised her freedom to choose to understand her mother from an alternative perspective, Clara felt lighter and freer, became less driven, and was more open to other people.

'The purpose of psychotherapy is to set people free', says May (1981, p. 19). Freedom, the existentialists note, necessarily includes both personal awareness and an understanding of the complexity of personal responsibility. In truth, the exercising of our freedom to choose is a hard path to follow. In reality, we are continually shifting across the divide of good and bad faith. Heidegger (1962), probably more realistically, describes that we are always in the process of becoming, that we move towards authenticity as we move towards our end. Mick Cooper captures this with his description of 'verb-like-ness' where 'existence is a verb-like process', a 'flux' (Merleau-Ponty, 1962), an 'unfolding event' (Hoffman, 1993), or 'path' (Jaspers, 1986) (in Cooper, 2016, p. 132). Freedom, too, is seen against the backdrop of the existential limitations of ontological givens such as death and our own facticity or the more personally limiting situations (Jaspers, 1986) – the confrontation of who we are and what we need to tackle in the face of dread, guilt, and anxiety. Indeed 'the basic step in achieving inward freedom is choosing one's self' (May, 1953, p. 125).

As Chapter 14 will show, who we are also includes a complex interplay of our mind and body, and the journey towards the freedom to choose one's self involves us attuning to the subtle and eloquent insights of the 'bodymind'.

14

Integrating Mind and Body

> Our body is not in space like things; it inhabits or haunts space. It applies itself to space like a hand to an instrument. And when we wish to move about, we do not move the body as we move an object.
>
> Merleau-Ponty, *The Primacy of Perception* (1964)

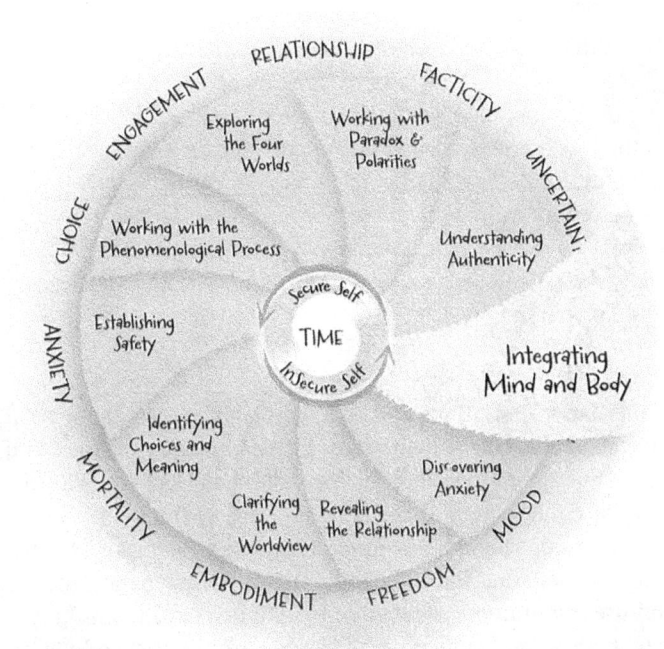

Source: Alison Strasser

Time-Limited Existential Therapy: The Wheel of Existence, Second Edition. Alison Strasser.
© 2022 John Wiley & Sons Ltd. Published 2022 by John Wiley & Sons Ltd.

Some people are inclined to use their rational mind to think and to analyse, tending to ignore how their bodies react or how their 'embodied being' is interacting and responding. Conversely, others may say that they rely on intuition, gut reactions or their emotional response to situations, potentially ignoring their reasoned responses. These differing patterns of reacting offer useful opportunities for exploration since they are often linked to learnt behaviour or beliefs that we hold dear. Considering the bodymind as a non-dualistic entity reveals a client's personal position and preference for their being-in-the-world.

> Martin not only wanted to stay in his thinking mind, but his body forced him to do so. Whenever he came close to noticing his feelings, he would unwittingly tap his head or flick his watchstrap against his wrist. He was so afraid of becoming like his 'crazy, emotional' mother that he had developed these strategies to protect him from feeling exposed to his feelings. He was thus successful in staying disconnected – and protected – from his feelings, his mother and from other intimate relationships.

> Conversely, Greg, who could talk about his anxiety, had, however, never made any connection to how his thoughts and feelings were being expressed in his body. He came to therapy because he had been experiencing physical symptoms which his doctors couldn't explain. As he talked about his anxiety, I began to direct his attention to his body. Greg noticed how his stomach and chest were pulsating. Like many clients, Greg found it easier to access his felt or body sense with his eyes closed. From this position, he could talk more explicitly about his worries and fears.

There are many alternative definitions and often conflicting views about what constitutes the mind, the body, and the emotions. In Asian languages, the word for *mind* and *heart* are the same. Cognitive behavioural therapists align with the scientific paradigm in its contention that changing the way we think has a direct effect on our actions and our feelings. In mindfulness, now taken up by CBT, mindfulness practitioners note that the body and mind are only separate entities in our thoughts and use mindfulness meditation to help us reveal the influence our thoughts have on bodies and emotions. Dan Siegel, a psychiatrist and neurobiologist, defines the mind 'as emerging in the transaction of at least neurobiological and interpersonal processes' (Siegel, 2007); he considers that it develops over our lifespan and that it is influenced by our complex arrangement of genes, neurons, synaptic connections, and our interpersonal experiences.

Like mindfulness and Buddhist philosophy, existential philosophy considers the mind and body, the bodymind, as a single entity and views the person as a unity, so that our knowing, our understanding, and our learning occur simultaneously with our minds and our bodies being inextricably bound together. There are no divisions of mind, thoughts, body, feelings, and emotions, although necessarily the divide is created through our language and our conversations. Spinelli (2015) describes how our experience is shaped 'cognitively, emotionally, and feelingly, as an overall "mood" expressive of a stance taken towards currently lived existence' (p. 63). The German word *Befindlichkeit*, used by Heidegger (1962) for 'state of mind' or 'how-one-finds-oneself', describes the way we take a stand, apprehend who we are, view others, and understand events. The understanding of experience in terms of 'how we find ourselves' is inclusive of the interconnectedness of mind and body.

Merleau-Ponty (1962) writes that all our consciousness is understood through our bodies, that our experience is embodied.

> If embodiment is an existential condition in which the body is the subjective source or intersubjective ground of experience, then studies under the rubric of embodiment are not 'about' the body per se. Instead they are about culture and experience insofar as these can be understood from the standpoint of bodily being-in-the-world. (in Csordas, 1994, p. 43)

This understanding has resonance with Eugene Gendlin's (1978) method of 'focusing', where our body is not an inert object but an experiential *process* that is continually interacting and responding to what is occurring in our world. It is the locus of our felt-sense whereby 'what we feel is not the inner content, but the sentience of what is happening in our living with others' (Madison, 2009, p. 7). Focusing is a process of flow where the person accesses their bodily experience, paying attention to their bodily sensations and, with their body, arriving at perspectives and meanings from a less cluttered, over-thinking, sense of knowing.

Even without explicitly using specific techniques such as focusing, therapists often sense the client's world through some form of bodily experience. For instance, as Martin talked, it slowly dawned on me that a tapping sensation was pulsating through my own body, similar to a knocking on the door. Instead of voicing this felt-sense to Martin, offering an explanation or inviting him to think about this experience, I asked him to pause, to notice what he was doing with his fingers and then close his eyes and describe what was happening in his body. He was surprised to notice that he could feel multiple sensations, including an image that revealed itself as a silver shield that he associated with a gladiator. Later, as he became more accustomed to his bodily sensations, he disclosed another image buried in his solar plexus region: a big black mesh that he referred to as fear. The tapping that I had experienced turned out to be one of the numerous diversional strategies he had developed to avert his feelings. Martin was in fear of 'overwhelm', certain that if he allowed his emotions to come to the fore, he would collapse and consequently find himself at risk of other people's vindictiveness. In an attempt to protect himself from this possibility he got into a habit of tapping his head or his feet, tugging at his elasticated watchstrap or any other object within his physical vicinity to ward off any rising emotion.

Integrating Emotions

As the bodymind is a unified entity, emotions and thoughts coexist and are made known and made clearer when working with our embodied understanding. Sartre (1957) writes that we are never without an emotion and emotions are always intentional or connected to some 'thing'. For example, an emotion such as anger is never directionless; on reflection, a particular event or sequence of events can be connected to the experience of anger. More often than not, emotions are both about the external event and inclusive of the personal response, the felt-sense. Emmy van Deurzen (2012) views emotions as our response to our values, so that anger might be one of the responses we experience if one of our values is under threat.

There is an increasing interest, in the therapeutic world, in what is currently referred to as the 'embodied theory of emotion'. This theory is now being confirmed by research in neuroscience, which 'looks at the [neural] connections between movement, cognition and emotion, along with the social context in which movement occurs. It views cognition as being shaped by bodily experience, that has itself been influenced by taking adaptive actions to meaningful aspects of the environment' (Hart, 2013).

As acknowledged by Cooper (2016) and others (Correia et al., 2018), there are many different 'schools' of existential therapy, and the practices of mindfulness and focusing are examples of philosophies that consider the individual as an integrated person. Our experiencing of ourselves, of others and of our surrounding environment encompasses more than thoughts, is more than words and includes our body:

> experiencing of the world is always and fundamentally somatic: . . . [the client] can never experience her world other than through her body. At every moment of her experiencing, her thoughts and her feelings are accompanied by ever-fluctuating internal and kinesthetic sensations, as well as by a sense of being in a body in a particular place in time. (Cooper, 2001, p. 5)

As the Wheel of Existence suggests, all our issues are interconnected. Using time and its inevitable limitation as an example, clients reveal their emotional state when confronted with the pressure of time. The careful tracking of our emotional responses helps identify and make connections to our personal principles; emotions disclose our worldview and self-esteem.

> Steve would drum his fingers on the arm of the sofa, expressing his frustration when he felt that I was taking away from his time in session by asking questions or making comments that he believed took him in a direction that he had not anticipated. He was determined to stay on track, to tell his story, and to feel in control. Eventually, after one of my interjections or questions, he expressed his disdain and found a way to criticise the existential approach or something I had said. These comments were directly related to the issue Steve had outlined in our first session: that he was both highly critical of others and always felt criticised, however much he thought he had done the right thing. It became clear that his desire to criticise others was a mechanism to stop his feelings of failure. His mother, who had mental health issues, would spend periods of time in hospital and, on her return, would criticise all his attempts to make her feel better. He couldn't understand why he was not loved and instead felt abandoned by his mother and others, feeling very isolated and alone.

While the time limitation, even within the session, and the impending separation, may create feelings of tension and stress, the therapist can work with what emerges and make deeper connections. Steve's fear of not having enough time in the session was linked to his sense that time would run out before receiving his mother's acknowledgement and love.

Emotions are complex and intricately entwined both with how we respond to our experiences and how these experiences influence the way we respond. As we all know, we often experience two or more voices that contradict each other. We can respond to situations from an almost childlike, unsophisticated, yearning position and simultaneously hear a more reasoned, rational internal voice say something else. Neither is right nor wrong, but both are worthy of exploration. These voices may reveal our hopes and aspirations as well as our fears and concerns and will disclose different aspects of our worldview. As described succinctly in his book on emotions, Strasser (1999) notes that we have both reflective and unreflective emotions. Reflective emotions are those that we can control. Unreflective emotions are hard to evaluate or even sense until we become aware of them. '[T]he process of therapy is, therefore, to facilitate the unreflective emotions to emerge into reflective ones' (1999, p. 27).

In the same way that our emotions mingle with our cognitions, our bodily responses have inner and outer expressions and, as we feel our emotions, so too will our body react. Often, we are not aware of this reaction unless we move into an obvious, full-blown bodily response such as panic. Our bodies will often react seemingly on their own accord, contradicting what our cognitive mind is saying. The clearing of our throat, a tapping of our feet, a flush, if we are unaware of them, are all examples of a possible disjunction between mind and body.

'Experience of our body is experience of our self, just as our thinking, imagery and ideas are part of our self' (Kepner, 1993, p. 10). It is always surprising, as we lean into ourselves, focusing in, the different responses that we hear. If we listen to our body-sense, we can hear other truths. The more we hear, the more we understand, the more we integrate, the more we take responsibility, the more we are in the 'becoming' – the more we are in our authentic being.

15

Understanding Authenticity

The only way to deal with an unfree world is to become so absolutely free that your very existence is an act of rebellion.

Albert Camus, *The Outsider* (1942)

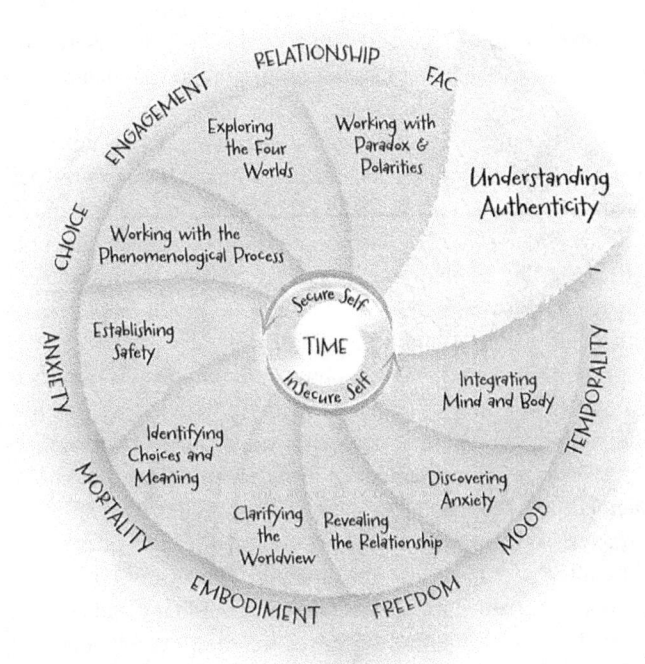

Source: Alison Strasser

Time-Limited Existential Therapy: The Wheel of Existence, Second Edition. Alison Strasser.
© 2022 John Wiley & Sons Ltd. Published 2022 by John Wiley & Sons Ltd.

Authenticity is not just a noun, nor a destination to be reached. It is closely aligned to the broader themes of awareness, choice, and freedom.

Kierkegaard (1992) claimed that the most common form of despair in not being who you are is a

> despair not to will to be oneself. Or even lower: in despair not to will to be a self. A self which has become a matter of calculation and management has ceased to be a self. It has become a thing. You must participate in a self in order to know what it is. (in Tillich, 1980, p. 124)

Authenticity, inauthenticity, bad faith, good faith are terms to describe our mode of existing in the world. I find the terms easier to understand when I consider them from the polarity of bad faith or the mode of inauthentic. These terms describe an existence whereby we are living a life defined by others' wishes, and include all the 'shoulds' and 'oughts' imposed by class, religion, and parental upbringing that pepper our lives. At the extreme, living inauthentically, or in bad faith, 'blinds' us to who we are and the effects we have on others and our environment.

Inauthenticity is a state (or *mode*) of being in which we deny or cut ourselves off from our own truth, a state in which we ignore our anxiety about the bigger existential givens of life, such as how we are living life, the risks that we take, our awareness of our temporality, our confrontation of our dying and what such anxiety may reveal. Inauthenticity also occurs when our belief and value systems (personal principles) get entrenched and sedimented to the extent that we are unable to see beyond what we believe is true. For Sartre, inauthenticity means living in bad faith such that 'through Bad Faith, a person seeks to escape the responsible freedom for being for itself' (Sartre, 1958, p. 629). Those living in bad faith are denying their freedom, their responsibility, and their anxiety.

Authenticity, on the other hand, in the philosophy of existentialism is a *mode of being* in which the features of self-awareness, responsibility, choice, action, and ultimately freedom are merged. Heidegger did not apply any value judgement to authenticity or inauthenticity, even to say that one mode of living is better than another: 'As modes of Being, *authenticity* and *inauthenticity* . . . are both grounded in the fact that any Dasein . . . is characterised by mineness. But the inauthenticity of Dasein does not signify any "less" Being or any "lower" degree of Being' (Heidegger, 1962, p. 68). We gain benefits from both authentic and inauthentic modes of being and both are required, depending on the context we find ourselves in. Paradoxically, knowing we're in an inauthentic space is in itself living in an authentic mode.

Authenticity is better understood as a verb that brings out the flexibility and flow that embraces living. Our capacity to maintain a quality of openness to the range of our ontic responses to the ontological givens of life facilitates a process of becoming authentic. As previously mentioned in Chapter 13, Mick Cooper (Cooper, 2016) describes this view as 'verb-like-ness'. This is also in keeping with Heidegger's (1962) understanding that we are 'always in the process of becoming' until the moment of our final breath. Indeed, we continually oscillate between authenticity and inauthenticity since there cannot be one state without the other. As such, authenticity is a theoretical notion and can never be achieved in its absolute form.

In *Being and Time* (1962), Heidegger explains that authenticity is the ability to stand on one's own, so that each person creates their own unique experience of life. As such, we are responsible for choosing our attitudes, making our decisions – even those such as facing our ultimate finitude. The path we choose is *our* path and ours alone. 'Authentic living is aware living' (van Deurzen & Adams, 2011, p. 92) and includes being present to all those ontological 'givens' that characterise our being between birth and death.

An authentic mode of being can be seen as acting from a state of being more 'true to oneself', where subsequent decisions are made through conscious awareness and where we are 'becoming increasingly capable of following the direction that one's conscience indicates as the right direction and thus becoming the author of one's own destiny' (van Deurzen, 2002, p. 43). To make authentic decisions means reviewing and sometimes discarding preconceived judgements and opinions imposed by society or significant figures and gaining insight into one's own intentions, purposes and inclinations. Conversely, we would define inauthentic behaviour as stemming from anxiety-driven, unreflective, out-of-awareness actions as well as the need to protect ourselves from the 'angst' of our very existence.

Indeed, an authentic approach may precipitate anxiety in our clients, as the crutches that have kept us safe and secure are being discarded. The therapist must guide the client to realise that it is a *sine qua non* to accept that existential anxiety or angst is not only part of life but the basic unease or malaise which humans experience as soon as they become aware of themselves. Existential anxiety is also, as previously stated, an ontological human characteristic.

The following case study will illustrate some of the interlinking themes that comprise the concept of authenticity, linking them back to the Wheel of Existence and the notion of responsibility, choice, and freedom.

> It was suggested by his coach that Laurie could benefit from learning more about his anxiety. Laurie was unhappily married with adult children and was getting ready to retire from a long and successful career in the financial sector. His job had taken him around the world, and he was well respected but did not feel particularly liked by his colleagues. He presented as having intense anxiety-related events, especially before going to sleep.
>
> Although Laurie was obviously in distress, I warmed to his sense of humour and knew that we would work together well.

Clarifying the Worldview/Sedimentation and Inauthenticity/Bad Faith (Chapters 11 and 15)

> Growing up as an only child on a remote property, Laurie spent many hours on his own, avoiding his often angry and violent father. He was home-schooled by his mother until, at the age of 11, he was sent to boarding school. Here, for the first time, he encountered other boys of his own age and learnt very quickly that his enquiring questions and bold comments were seen as spitefully critical. He didn't know how to make friends and found it easier to exclude himself, withdrawing into his imaginative world of fantasy novels. His sedimented stance was that it was best to remain withdrawn and removed from people because the opposite, the polarity of being curious and outgoing, had devastating repercussions of feeling like an outcast, a person of reprehensible motivations.
>
> At university, Laurie met Rose whom he thought was an ideal partner because she was emotionally distanced and didn't make any demands on him. He thought that Rose's lack of emotions was a more mature way of living and he set about advancing his career. He didn't notice or think about the fact that there was little intimacy in their relationship and their social life was non-existent. On the positive side, Laurie rose quickly to become a senior executive and the family travelled and lived in many of the key global cities.
>
> Although proficient at his job, Laurie was upsetting his key staff through his lack of emotional connection. He was allocated a coach to help his communication skills and it was at that point that he began to realise how much he had excommunicated his emotional world.
>
> By the time I saw Laurie, several years later, he had learnt how to develop rapport with his colleagues and was able to watch and witness his own behaviours and thought patterns. He had one further year before retiring and he was anxious about this prospect and what he would do with his time. The first few sessions were taken up with his desire to separate from Rose. Five years previously, they had agreed to part ways, but nothing had changed and life continued as before. We explored the reasons for Laurie resisting change and staying with the status quo, until he realised that he was more concerned about not upsetting Rose than taking note of his personal needs and desire for a different, more emotionally connected life.
>
> In many respects, Laurie lived a good life. However, it was in hindsight that he realised that, in certain aspects of his life, he had been living inauthentically: it had been easier for him to live in a marriage with little intimacy so that he didn't have to confront feelings of inferiority, rejection, anger, or the sadness that he'd had to navigate as a child. There's no magic switch from bad to good faith or from inauthentic to authentic living but, through his growing awareness, Laurie was able to make a different choice.

Identifying Choices and Meaning, and Freedom
(Chapters 13 and 5)

This process of increasing awareness brings us to a more authentic and personally informed existence. As we reach into our self-awareness, we can appreciate how our personal principles have guided our existence, sometimes in directions that may have safeguarded us as children but have limited our patterns of emotional and behavioural responses as adults.

> From the age of 11, if not before, Laurie had chosen to keep people at a distance. His experience with his fellow schoolmates was life shattering and skewed most of his relationships for many years. It is true, too, that life is not black and white, and Laurie had experienced moments of closeness with friends. He was a keen tennis player and, as part of the team, had developed friendships with other men who accepted him as a recluse, joining in social activities when it suited.
>
> Within 3 months of starting therapy, Rose and Laurie had found separate places to live; their parting was amicable. His choice to leave the relationship was a choice to find a new way of living. Freedom from his sedimented stance had a double benefit in that it also brought forth his freedom towards another way of being. Laurie was prepared to face his vulnerability and was excited, too, at the possibility of exploring his more outgoing side that he had suppressed in his childhood.

Awareness is only the first step in therapy and is hopefully followed by choice and actions. Even a *choice* to remain the same is a choice that paradoxically involves change.

> Laurie was a man of action and once he had realised that he wanted to live his future life differently, he took the necessary steps. He found himself a small inner-city house that suited his wish to explore different communities and friendship groups. He wasn't averse to finding a new partner so that he could get to know what it was like to feel close to someone with whom he had an intimate connection.

As discussed previously, freedom has both possibilities and limitations. Indeed, after Laurie and Rose parted, he was startled to find that he was experiencing more anxiety.

Discovering Anxiety (Chapter 8)

> Sitting on the edge of the sofa, Laurie admitted that he had wanted to cancel our session. He was wondering whether therapy itself was making him feel more anxious.

This was not the first time I have heard this said, and my sense is that it's not necessarily that we become more anxious during therapy, but that we are more able to be attuned to, and describe, our anxiety.

> The session wasn't easy. Laurie's anxiety heightened as he spoke. He didn't want me to look at him because it made him feel anxious, exposed.
>
> As Laurie's story unfolded, he remembered being scared of his grandfather who came to live with them when he was 5. This grandfather would appear seemingly from nowhere and Laurie's fear was exacerbated when his mother told him to avoid him. At night, he would lie in his darkened room in the full belief that his grandfather would burst into his bedroom and do something dreadful. Although he couldn't describe what this dastardly deed might be, in the early stages of his therapy he resumed a night-time ritual, which had begun in his childhood, of checking under the bed, in the wardrobes and behind the curtains to ensure that he was alone and not about to be sprung on. Laurie now realised that variations of these behaviours continued to the current day, including hooking a chair underneath the doorknob when staying in hotels.
>
> Ultimately, after listening to and exploring Laurie's story and his felt-sense of his experience, a common factor appeared as a long-seated fear of being attacked either physically or emotionally. This tied in with his sedimentation that if he was gregarious and curious, he would be attacked, and his ultimate fear was of his own physical and spiritual annihilation.

Identifying Choices and Meaning/Responsibility and Authenticity (Chapters 13 and 15)

Responsibility is more than the sum of our own actions and necessarily includes our behaviours with others and towards the environment around us. In therapy, we are on a journey towards good faith or authenticity, requiring us to become more mindful of our actions and their consequences.

> Significant to Laurie's journey was the recognition that he did have needs and wants, separate to what he gained from his work environment. Once he saw that separating from his wife would also benefit Rose, he began to concentrate on his emotional world, beginning with his two adult children. As an 'absent' father during their early years, he had friendly but distant relationships with both his son and daughter. He took it upon himself to spend more time with each, and to not only learn about their lives but also share his world and his vulnerabilities with them. Laurie started laughing more, amused at his own inadequacies, such as his attempts at cooking or joining book clubs. His anxiety also lessened, and he could retire to bed without his elaborate checking rituals.

In this process of recognition and understanding we are on our path to *becoming*, our path towards authenticity, our path towards becoming responsible and taking responsibility. Nietzsche also views responsibility and freedom as taking charge of our lives, while Kierkegaard links choice and action, in that it's not just about our ability to choose but, rather, choosing is man's 'responsibility for the manner of his existence' (1992, p. 54).

Time and Temporality (Chapters 3 and 5)

> The initial therapy contract with Laurie was to periodically review his progress so as to take care of a timely ending. After separating from Rose and moving into his new house, Laurie admitted fretting, convinced that I would want to end our sessions.

Endings are such a poignant aspect of our human existence and become imbued with a variety of individual meanings, ranging from fear of abandonment and annihilation to fear of attachment and dependency. We all know that endings (and beginnings) are inevitable and we both crave and get anxious about the inescapable changes that will occur.

> Laurie had discovered different friendship groups and was also exploring our relationship. He was frightened that he might have overstepped the therapeutic boundaries when he offered to give me some theatre tickets. Although I attempted to be gentle in my refusal, he took this rebuttal as a rejection and

> felt as if the sword of Damocles was hanging over his head, anticipating my rejection.
>
> This series of events was an opportunity for Laurie to gain a greater understanding of his sedimentation and to consider his polarity of being withdrawn versus being outgoing from a more reflective, adult perspective. He realised, by considering our interactions, that he could adopt different approaches and styles of engagement in the way he expressed his curiosity about other people and the way he questioned ideas. Laurie could still satisfy his interest by assuming a gentler, more hesitant style, thereby not causing offence to others.
>
> We didn't end at this point but continued for another 9 months. During this time, we also explored the significance of Laurie's pending retirement and the reality of his age. This returned us to his initial presenting anxiety related to his going to sleep, which now he could see was also linked to his fear of his ultimate end, his death.
>
> Our last session was sad for both of us. Laurie had challenged my professional boundaries and I empathised with his struggle to find a more authentic and meaningful life for himself without the structures of marriage or work. And now, he was striding forth without the anchor of his therapist. It takes courage to enter into therapy and courage to end.

As we finish describing authenticity, we have come full circle on the Wheel of Existence. As we can now see, to deny or avoid the limitations inherent in our lives is to deny or avoid the 'what is', and thus to live in what Sartre deemed to be bad faith.

Taking up our responsibility, however, cannot occur in a state of 'blindness' or bad faith (Sartre, 1958) or inauthenticity (Heidegger, 1962). With the process of recognition and understanding we become more mindful of our actions and their consequences and find ourselves on our path to *becoming*. Each of the sections of the Wheel provides a way of understanding ourselves, of achieving a more enlightened awareness and helping us carve out a path to more authentic thinking.

It might be obvious that we are always in time, but until we stop and reflect about what time is and how it relates to our everyday sense of being alive, we seem to literally allow time to run its own course. A paradox, yes, in that time inevitably is its own destiny and cascades forwards without our input; yet the significance of reflecting on how time impacts us within every miniscule moment illuminates the very essence of what our past, present, and future time can awaken within us. One of the most primary reminders noted by Heidegger is that, from the moment we enter into the world, we also know that we are going to exit – we are all going to die. Or, all beginnings are intertwined with endings. This one essential given provides an overarching and all-encompassing mantle over our existence. It is how we each respond to this particular given that is at the heart of this time-limited approach to therapy.

As we follow the path of authenticity, the choices, indeed *within* the limitations of the existential 'givens', become more apparent. Thus, the journey towards authenticity, which includes facing our facticity, our anxiety, our mortality, our moods, the uncertainty of living, an understanding of the complexity of responsibility and ultimately the making of authentic choices, all within the context of the temporality of our existence, is also a journey towards our freedom.

> In my beginning is my end. In succession
> Houses rise and fall, crumble, are extended,
> Are removed, destroyed, restored, or in their place
> Is an open field, or a factory, or a by-pass.
> Old stone to new building, old timber to new fires,
> Old fires to ashes, and ashes to the earth. (Eliot, 1943)

Afterword: COVID-19

(April 2020)

> *The line, it is drawn, the curse, it is cast.*
> *The slow one now will later be fast.*
> *As the present now will later be past.*
> *The order is rapidly fading.*
> *And the first one now will later be last.*
> *For the times, they are a-changin'.*
>
> Bob Dylan, *The Times They Are a-Changin'*, 1964

As I was about to commence the fourth draft of this book, Easter 2020, the gnawing signs of the COVID-19 virus that had been rumbling on the edges of my awareness, erupted into full consciousness. Australia closed its borders to the rest of the world, and we were forced into physical isolation. The stories of inadequate medical resources, unprepared governments and raw footage of people being starved of oxygen was torturous to comprehend. I roamed around my house in disbelief, wanting to watch/listen/read about what was happening while simultaneously noting my propensity to withdraw from the world.

My disbelief and my yearning to disengage were quickly replaced with a sense of wonder and curiosity when I began to realise that the theme of this book and the thesis of the limitation of time in the therapy room was being played out in front of my eyes. COVID-19 was the catalyst for change.

The advent of COVID-19 and the responses by governments have created a 'limit' to how we live our lives in a manner similarly impactful to that imposed by the time limit in therapy and the foreknowledge that everything comes to an end in our lives, which culminate in our own deaths.

This new virus was and still is taking the world by surprise, not only in its unique viral composition and its impact on the human body, but also in how

Time-Limited Existential Therapy: The Wheel of Existence, Second Edition. Alison Strasser.
© 2022 John Wiley & Sons Ltd. Published 2022 by John Wiley & Sons Ltd.

this unparalleled global lockdown is truly mirroring the existential themes written about in this book. I've found that using the Wheel of Existence in my practice gives me an overall understanding of the interplay of the ontological givens and ontic responses as well as where to navigate or focus in on a client's worldview.

Anxiety is at the fore of everyone's experience. In line with all major disruptions in life, in response to which humans tend to fight, flee or freeze, my first response was to freeze. This was replaced by a determination to find any means possible to retain a semblance of the life I had just lost. I became a Zoom junkie, doubling my yoga classes, having online drinks with friends, actively creating workshops for my business and so on. All my client and supervision work were now online. I was utilising lost skills from my earlier TV career and jumping headlong into a new world. Yes, very exciting and creative. In hindsight, this keen enthusiasm was both a means to keep my sense of aliveness blooming, and also a means to shift my emotional world away from the bleakness of uncertainty to something more solid and certain.

Similarly, my night-time dreams and my anxiousness upon waking spoke to me from a position of existential dread. There was a more acute 'knowing' of the finality of the life that I had created and a more heightened sensation of death – yes, that of myself, family, and friends but also the multitude of grieving people around the world who were living in various states of shock and despair. This period has been and continues to be a major confrontation with death – our own, others' – and loss, of our daily routines and future dreams.

All this brings life into sharper focus: all the conversations we should have had, the projects that were never completed, the acts of kindness that remained merely as thoughts.

As I continue to work with clients and supervisees, I am also sitting in wonder at how the limitations brought about by the pandemic are bringing about a renewed understanding of freedom. Those of us in the developed world had so much choice at the press of a button: we could travel the world, shop amongst a myriad of brand selections in the supermarket and other stores, dine out or in, spend time with friends or not. Yet, many of us are finding that sitting with less is a relief. We are realising that coping with the external pressures of having to do something or be somewhere is exhausting. It's as if we were so caught up with the 'shoulds' and 'oughts' of existence that we had little idea of the alternative. The virus has given individuals, families, governments, and societies an opportunity to change our 'rules' or challenge our sedimented beliefs, with the possibility of living life more courageously.

> In a Zoom session 2 weeks into lockdown, Laura, a well-mannered 32-year-old actress who doesn't like to upset people, described how she had spoken to her agent, wanting answers to questions about her career that she had always wanted to ask but had resisted for fear of offending her agent. Laura's appreciation that her agent has to face the identical issues as she does, and her acknowledgement of their having to confront the same horrors, helped her to dismantle her previously held belief in her agent's superiority and see that her agent was no better than her, but equal in terms of their shared experience of the same enemy – the COVID-19 virus – as well as someone who has different skills, which enabled Laura to advance her career.

As a visible and tangible threat to our very existence, the virus has, at least temporarily, helped to shift our attitude to our internal sedimented principles.

I, too, find myself more aligned with my fellow human beings and I've noticed that I'm more likely to talk about what is happening in the wider world and give more time to hearing about our mutual experiences. These conversations feel more equal, human, and beautifully humane. Clients reply with their personal stories and intimate responses.

The central theme of time still plays its personal tune but it has become sharply more noticeable. As everyday routines have changed, so have people's relationship to time. Many people are finding a different daily rhythm as they realise how much time was taken up in the preparations for, and travel time in, getting children to school and themselves to work. As one client, Sarah, said, 'I'm liking this; I feel that for the first time since I can remember, I have space to breathe. There's a whole lot of things I now don't have to do. I never realised how many "shoulds" were in my life.'

> Another client, Jeremy, explained that his main reason for coming to therapy was his tumultuous marriage, his exasperation with his wife and his dread of what might happen to his dream of a family life. At the onset of the COVID-19 virus, Jeremy and his partner found themselves working at home with their 7-year-old daughter. As Jeremy's pressure of time eased, he found a 'kinder' space within himself and a greater willingness to listen to his partner. He added a meditation routine to his day and structured in playtime with his daughter before breakfast. He and his partner were able to talk through how to share the home schooling in accordance with both their work schedules. Jeremy's natural wish to care had found a new home.

Personal and social rules are being broken. There is a visible pause in the relentless noisiness of the busy world; it's as if COVID-19 has provided the excuse.

> David, who now lives in San Francisco, was terrified as a child that his parents would be infected with his 'gayness', so he withdrew, only revealing the parts of himself that he felt were socially acceptable. He has thoroughly embraced the lockdown: 'I'm happy in my isolation, in fact happier than I've ever been. I've always felt isolated, or rather I chose isolation to protect others from my badness. Now, life has met me in my place. For the first time, I know that I have friends but, more than that, others now have to play by my rules, so "welcome to the party".'

Interestingly, the constraints brought about by COVID-19 have heightened people's awareness of what is meaningful. Supervisees talk about clients who have decided to change professions and pursue ideas that were previously only wild dreams.

> Marian would beam in her weekly Zoom sessions as she exuberantly spoke about the play she was writing. Previously, I would have described her as a very talented woman, but unmotivated and sad. She managed to finish writing and directed an online reading of the play using actors working from home. Her happiness is contagious. In contrast to her previous apathy, Marian had discovered her creativity when curbs and restrictions had been imposed on her.

'He who has a *why* to live can bear with almost any *how*' – this is a very apt phrase from Nietzsche, much quoted by Frankl (1963, p. 46).

Likewise, COVID-19 seems to have provided the motive to implement changes that have lain dormant, the will to speak the unutterable and the motivation to be inspirational at the level of government. I'm amused by our Australian government which appears to be taking the opportunity to put into action changes that have been long discussed, such as the antiquated tax system and the greening of our energy supply – changes that on the surface could bring about social change and benefit the wider Australian community.

Although we cognitively know that the future is unknown and unpredictable, we tend to prepare for life as if this is not true. As one of life's paradoxes, we need a sense of future time to propel and to grow towards our dreams. The shock of the pandemic is that the immediate sense of any future that we've created is lost and we are stumbling blindly in the dark. The future is now really unknown. We watch and wait for the ever-changing statistics of the infected and the dead, clinging to the hope that the decrease in numbers will return us to a past that is no longer there.

The future, however, will never be the same. Sometimes known as the liminal space (Van Gennep, 1960), it is the transitional space we find ourselves inhabiting when we're transported out of a particular known set of circumstances into an unknown place. In this kind of lifeworld disruption, is both a loss of what we have known and a sense of possibility as we look towards the future. In this liminal space, we go through various stages, starting with the sense of uncertainty or ambiguity and moving into the passage of possibility where we learn to navigate and adapt to new norms, rules, and values, before shifting into the third state where we begin to integrate into the new norms.

At the start, we may have to stare into a void. Existentially, we're sitting in the possibility of becoming without knowing how this might turn out to be.

> Daniel had led an eventful life, had spent many years attending self-healing workshops and had learnt many strategies for avoiding anxiety. The COVID-19 lockdown was serendipitous in that earlier events in his life were returning to haunt his waking and sleeping life and now for the first time he felt different. He laughed as he described 'leaning into the void', the place that he had run away from for years, and in which he now discovered, not the emptiness that he dreaded, but a space where he felt connected to himself and others.

And we adapt. Change is inevitable even in times of chronic crisis and we adapt to what has become known facetiously as the 'new normal'. Six months into COVID, there is still a feeling of unsettledness. The initial hope that it would all be over within 6 months has faded into the background but the desire for a future is still palpable. Repeated phrases and conversations reiterate a prospect of a vaccine and the reasoned rationale of living with this virus as we've learnt to live with other viruses – all examples that take away the personal terror of the COVID statistics of suffering and death.

As the dust settles, there's also a restlessness, a paradoxical tug around personal freedoms versus the good of the community. We're more isolated and yet remarkably connected. Time has taken on new dimensions. Working at home, practising social distancing, and only leaving home for exercise has had an impact on our sense of order. Hours of the day and even days of the week are merging. We are learning not to plan, or at least to hold our future very lightly. We're learning to see and live within the existential limitations that are always there but not always so visible.

The existential givens are alive and kicking. The ontic hums of existence are no longer buzzing in the background but are now hissing in the foreground, unable to be ignored. 'In the midst of beings as a whole an open place occurs. There is a clearing' (Heidegger, 1962, p. 51). Heidegger's push towards authentic living and Sartre's (1958) appreciation of bad faith are now lit up. This current sense of space and time that is dominated by COVID-19 is a coming home to ourselves, to a 'sitting' with the existential truth of what 'is'.

References

Adams, D. (1975) *The hitchhiker's guide to the galaxy: A trilogy in five parts*. London: William Heinemann.

Adams, M. (2013) *A concise introduction to existential counselling*. London: Sage.

Anderson, A. A., Hicks, S. V. & Witkowski, L. (Eds) (2004) *Mythos & logos: How to regain the love of wisdom*. Amsterdam: Rodopi.

Baldwin, M. (2000) *Interview with Carl Rogers on the use of self in therapy*. (M. Baldwin, Ed.). New York: Haworth.

Binswanger, L. (1963) *Being-in-the-world*. (J. Needleman, Trans. & Ed.). New York: BasicBooks.

Borges, J. L. (1964) *Labyrinths: Selected stories and other writings*. New York: New Directions.

Bowen, M., & Cooper, M. (2012) Development of a client feedback tool: A qualitative study of therapists' experiences of using the Therapy Personalisation. *European Journal of Psychotherapy Counselling and Health, 14*, 47–62.

Buber, M. (1970) *I and thou*. Edinburgh: T&T Clark.

Buber, M. (1990) Martin Buber. In *Carl Rogers Dialogues* (H. Kirschenbaum & V. L. Henderson, Eds) (pp. 41–63). London: Constable & Company.

Camus, A. (1942) *The outsider*. New York: Penguin.

Camus, A. (1984) *The myth of Sisyphus*. New York: Penguin.

Chambers 21st Century Dictionary. (2021) https://chambers.co.uk.

Cohn, H. (1997) *Existential thought and therapeutic practice: An introduction to existential psychotherapy*. London: Sage.

Cooper, M. (2001) Embodied empathy. In S. Haugh & T. Merry (Eds), *Empathy* (pp. 218–229). Ross-on-Wye: PCCS Books.

Cooper, M. (2003) *Existential therapies*. London: Sage.

Cooper, M. (2016) *Existential therapies* (2nd ed.). London: Sage.

Cooper, M., & Mearns, D. (2005) *Working at relational depth in counselling and psychotherapy*. London: Sage.

Cooper, M., & Spinelli, E. (2012) A dialogue on dialogue. In L. Barnett & G. Madison (Eds), *Existential therapy: Legacy, vibrancy and dialogue*. Hove: Routledge.

Correia, E. A., Cooper, M. & Berdondini, L. (2014) Existential psychotherapy: An international survey of the key authors and texts influencing practice. *Journal of Contemporary Psychotherapy*. doi: 10.1007/s10879-014-9275-y.

Correia, E. A., Sartóris, V., Fernandes, T., Cooper, M., Berdondini, L., Sousa, D., . . . da Fonseca, J. (2018) The practices of existential psychotherapists: Development and application of an observational grid. *British Journal of Guidance & Counselling*, 42(2), 201–216.

Craig, E. (2008) The human and the hidden: Existential wonderings about depth, soul and the unconscious. *The Humanistic Psychologist*, 36(3), 227–282.

Critchley, S. (2009) Being and Time, Part 4: Thrown into this world. Retrieved from http://www.theguardian.com/commentisfree/belief/2009/jun/29/religion-philosophy (accessed 21/3/2017).

Csordas, T. J. (1994) *Embodiment and experience: The existential ground of culture and self*. Cambridge: Cambridge University Press

De Shazer, S. & Dolan, Y. with Korman, H., Trepper, T. S., McCollom, E. & Berg, I. K. (2007) *More than miracles: The state of the art of solution-focused brief therapy*. Binghamtom, NY: Haworth Press.

Deurzen, E. van (1988) *Existential counselling & psychotherapy in practice*. London: Sage.

Deurzen, E. van (1997) *Everyday mysteries: Existential dimensions of psychotherapy*. London: Routledge.

Deurzen, E. van (2002) *Existential counselling & therapy in practice*. London: Sage.

Deurzen, E. van (2010) *Everyday mysteries: A handbook of existential psychotherapy* (2nd ed.). London: Routledge.

Deurzen, E. van (2012) *Existential counselling & psychotherapy in practice* (3rd ed.). London: Sage.

Deurzen, E. van (2014) Structural existential analysis (SEA): A phenomenological method for therapeutic work. *Journal of Contemporary Psychotherapy*, 45, 59–68. (Online 21 September 2014).

Deurzen, E. van, & Adams, M. (2011) *Skills in existential counselling & psychotherapy*. London: Sage.

Deurzen, E. van, & Arnold Baker, C. (2019) Existential-phenomenological therapy illustration: Rahim's dilemma. In E. van Deurzen (Ed.), *The Wiley world handbook of existential therapy*. Chichester: Wiley.

Duncan, B., Miller, S., Wampold, B., & Hubble, M. (2010) *The heart and soul of change: Delivering "what works" in therapy*. Washington, DC: American Psychological Association.

References

Eliot, T. S. (1943) *Four quartets*. New York: Harcourt, Brace and Company.
Frankl, V. E. (1963) *Man's search for meaning*. New York: Pocket Books.
Gendlin, E. T. (1978) *Focusing*. New York: Bantam.
Gibran, K. (1923) *The prophet*. New York: Alfred A. Knopf.
Greenson, R. (1967) *The technique and practice of psychoanalysis*. London: Hogarth Press.
Guignon, C. (2009) The body, bodily feelings, and existential feelings: A Heideggerian perspective. *Philosophy, Psychiatry, & Psychology*, *16*(2), 195–199.
Halling, S., & Goldfarb, M. (1991) Grounding truth in the body: Therapy and research renewed. *The Humanistic Psychologist*, *19*(3), 313–330.
Hart, C. (2013) Held in mind, out of awareness: Perspectives on the continuum of dissociated experiences culminating in dissociative identity disorder in children. *Journal of Child Psychotherapy*, *39*(3). Published online 23 October 2013.
Heidegger, M. (1962) *Being and time*. Oxford: Basil Blackwell.
Hoffman, L. (2015). The 'new' in the New Existentialists: Embracing paradox. In *Conference: World Congress of Existential Therapy*. London.
Hoffman, P. (1993) Death, time, history: Division II of Being and Time. In C. Guignon (Ed.), *The Cambridge companion to Heidegger's Being and Time*. Cambridge: Cambridge University Press.
Husserl, E. (1970) *Logical investigations* (J. N Findlay, Trans.). New York: Humanities Press.
Husserl, E. (1977) *Phenomenological psychology*. The Hague: Nijhoff.
Ihde, D. (1986) *Experimental phenomenology*. Albany: State University of New York Press.
Jaspers, K. (1932) *Philosophie*. Berlin: Springer.
Jaspers, K. (1963) *General psychopathology* (trans. from German by J. Hoenig & M. W. Hamilton, Ed.). Manchester: Manchester University Press.
Jaspers, K. (1986) *Karl Jaspers: Basic philosophical writings*. (L. H. E. and G. B. P., Trans., E. Ehrkich, Ed.). Atlantic Highlands, NJ: Humanities Press.
Jourard, S. M. (1971) *The transparent self*. New York: Van Nostrand Reinhold.
Kepner, J. I. (1993) *Body process: Working with the body in psychotherapy*. San Francisco: Jossey-Bass.
Khong, B. (2013) Being a therapist: Contribution of Heidegger's philosophy and the Buddha's teachings to psychotherapy. *The Humanistic Psychologist*, *41*, 231–246.
Kierkegaard, S. (1941) *Concluding unscientific postscript* (D. F. Swenson, Trans.). Princeton, NJ: Princeton University Press.
Kierkegaard, S. (1967) *Philosophical fragments*. Princeton NJ: Princeton University Press.
Kierkegaard, S. (1989) *The sickness unto death: A Christian psychological exposition of edification and awakening by anti-Climacus*. London: Penguin.
Kierkegaard, S. (1992) *Either/or: A fragment of life*. London: Penguin Classics.

References

Koontz, D. (1979) *The key to midnight*. New York: Pocket Books.
Kubrick, S. (2001) *Stanley Kubrick Interviews* (G. D. Phillips, Ed.). Jackson: University Press of Mississippi.
Lacan, J. (1998) *The four fundamental concepts of psychoanalysis*. New York: W. W. Norton.
Lamont, N. (2012) The end in sight. *Existential Analysis, 23*(January), 89–100.
Langdridge, D. (2013) *Existential counselling and psychotherapy*. London: Sage.
Längle, A. (2015) From Viktor Frankl's logotherapy to existential analytic psychotherapy. *European Psychotherapy, 9*(1), 67–83.
Levinas, E. (1998) *Totality and infinity: An essay on exteriority*. Ann Arbor, MI: Duquesne University Press.
Levinas, E. (2006) *Humanism of the other* (N. Poller, Trans., Ed.). Montpellier: Editions Fata Morgana.
Madison, G. (2009) Evocative supervision. In E. van Deurzen & S. Young (Eds), *Existential perspectives on supervision* (pp. 185–196). Basingstoke: Palgrave Macmillan.
Madison, G. (2010) Focusing on existence: Five facets of an experiential-existential model. *Person-Centred and Experiential Psychotherapies, 9*(23), 189–204.
Maslow, A. (1968) *Towards a psychology of being*. New York: Van Nostrand Reinhold.
May, R. (1953) *Man's search for himself*. New York: W. W. Norton.
May, R. (1961) *Existential psychology*. New York: Random House.
May, R. (1967) *Psychology and the human dilemma*. New York: W. W. Norton.
May, R. (1981) *Freedom and destiny*. New York: W. W. Norton.
May, R. (1983) *The discovery of being: Writings in existential psychology*. New York: W. W. Norton.
May, R. (1991) *The cry for myth*. New York: W. W. Norton.
Merleau-Ponty, M. (1962) *The phenomenology of perception* (C. Smith, Trans.). London: Routledge & Kegan Paul.
Merleau-Ponty, M. (1964) *The primacy of perception* (C. Smith, Trans., Ed.). New York: Humanities Press.
Merriam Webster Dictionary (2021) https://www.merriam-webster.com/dictionary/sediment (accessed 28/2/2021).
Nanda, J. (2009) Mindfulness: A lived experience of existential-phenomenological themes. *Existence A New Dimension in Psychiatry and Psychology, 20*(1)(January), 147–163.
Nietzche, F. (1974) *The gay science* (W. Kaufmann, Trans., Ed.). New York: Vintage.
O'Dowd, W. T. (1986) Otto Rank and time-limited psychotherapy. *Psychotherapy, 23*(1), 140–149.
Rank, O. (1929) *The trauma of birth*. New York: Harcourt Brace.
Rogers, C. (1961) *On becoming a person*. London: Constable.
Rogers, C. (1980) *A way of being*. Boston, MA: Houghton Mifflin.

References

Rumi. (1993) *The love poems of Rumi* (D. Chopra, Ed.). London: Rider.

Sartre, J.-P. (1957) *Existentialism and human emotions* (B. Frechtman, Trans.). New York: Philosophical Lib. Retrieved from http://www.philosophymagazine.com/others/MO_Sartre_Existentialism.htm.

Sartre, J.-P. (1958) *Being and nothingness: An essay in phenomenological ontology*. London: Routledge.

Sartre, J.-P. (1973) *Existentialism is a humanism*. London: Methuen.

Schneider, K. J., & Krug, O. T. (2010). *Existential-humanistic therapy*. Washington, DC: American Psychological Association.

Siegel, D. (2007) An interpersonal neurobiology approach to psychotherapy: Awareness, mirror neurons, and neural plasticity in the development of well-being. Retrieved from http://www.ithou.org/node/2730 (accessed 30/1/2015).

Spinelli, E. (1989) *The interpreted world: An introduction to phenomenological psychology. booksgooglecom* (2nd ed.). London: Sage.

Spinelli, E. (1994) *Demystifying therapy*. London: Constable.

Spinelli, E. (2001) *The mirror and the hammer: Challenges to therapeutic orthodoxy*. London: Sage.

Spinelli, E. (2006) Existential psychotherapy : An introductory overview. *Análise Psicológica*, *3*, 311–321.

Spinelli, E. (2007) *Practising existential therapy: The relational world*. London: Sage.

Spinelli, E. (2015) *Practicing existential therapy: The relational world* (2nd ed.). London: Sage.

Spinelli, E. (2016). Experiencing change: An existential perspective. In S. Schulenberg (Ed.), *Clarifying and furthering existential psychotherapy: Theories, methods and practices* (pp. 131–142). Cham: Springer.

Stern, D. (2004) *The present moment in psychotherapy and everyday life*. New York: W. W. Norton.

Stolorow, G., & Atwood, E. (2016). Walking the tightrope of emotional dwelling. *Psychoanalytic Dialogues*, *26*(1), 103–108.

Strasser, A. (2004) *Development of a counselling and psychotherapy supervision training program within an Australian educational context* (Doctoral dissertation, Middlesex Univesity). Retrieved from https://eprints.mdx.ac.uk/6437/1/Strasser_Development_of_a_counselling_and_psychotherapy_programme.pdf.

Strasser, F. (1999) *Emotions: Experiences in existential psychotherapy and life*. London: Duckworth.

Strasser, F., & Strasser, A. (1997) *Existential time-limited therapy: The wheel of existence*. Chichester: Wiley.

Stravinski, I. (1970). *Poetics of music in the form of six lessons* (O. Ponsatí-Murlà trans, Ed.). Boston, MA: Harvard University Press.

Taft, J. (1933) *The dynamics of therapy in a controlled relationship*. New York: Dover.

The Free Dictionary (2021) Paradox. https://www.thefreedictionary.com/paradox (accessed 1/2/2021).
Tillich, P. (1980) *The courage to be*. New York: Yale University Press.
Van Gennep (1960) *Les rites de passage*. Chicago: Chicago University Press.
Wahl, J. (2003) Working with 'existence tension' as a basis for therapeutic practice. *Journal for the Society of Existential Analysis*, 4(2), 265–278.
Warnock, M. (1970) *Existentialism*. Oxford: Oxford University Press.
Yalom, I. (1980) *Existential psychotherapy*. New York: Basic Books.
Yalom, I. (2008) *Staring at the sun: Overcoming the terror of death*. London: Piatkus.

Index

a
absurdity   136
aloneness   4, 35, 55, 78, 118
anxiety
  ending   91
  existential   47, 82, 90, 149
  ontological   51, 82
approach
  brief   33
  modular   34–37
  open-ended   26, 30, 32, 37
  time aware   27, 35, 80
  time-limited   30, 36–38, 155
assessment   25, 36, 37
assumptions   58, 59, 61, 62, 67, 69, 71, 113, 116
attitude   4, 8, 12, 18, 24, 31, 51, 57, 59, 60, 63, 68, 70–72, 89, 92, 116, 138, 158
authenticity
  and anxiety   148
  inauthenticity   82, 148–150, 154
  in relationships   150, 151
awareness
  self   92, 148, 151

b
Bad Faith   148

becoming   58, 65, 89, 92, 114, 130, 133, 139, 142, 146, 148, 153, 154, 160, 187
Befindlichkeit   143
beginnings   12, 15, 20, 21, 25, 31, 46, 76, 79, 153, 154
being-in-the-world   5, 7–9, 45, 48, 54, 55, 92, 94, 103, 105, 133, 142, 143
being-towards-death   46, 47
being-unto-death, xiv
being-with-others   45, 95, 103
belief system   31, 109, 119, 128, 129
bias   61, 62
Binswanger, L.   15, 105
biological time   105
body
  bodyhood   89
  bodymind   140, 142–144
  body self   49
Boundaries   25, 75, 77, 153, 154
bracketing (epoquē)   59, 61
brief therapy   32–34, 77
Buber, M.   64, 95, 97, 100
Buddhism   110, 143

c
Camus, A.   133, 135, 136, 147

Time-Limited Existential Therapy: The Wheel of Existence, Second Edition. Alison Strasser.
© 2022 John Wiley & Sons Ltd. Published 2022 by John Wiley & Sons Ltd.

certainty 6, 22, 31, 47, 50, 51, 58, 74, 80, 83, 86, 113, 115, 117, 124, 133
challenge/challenging 24, 60, 62, 64, 67–68, 70, 116
change 6, 7, 13, 16, 18, 21, 23, 24, 33–35, 37, 46, 51, 58, 59, 66, 77, 80, 82, 89, 97, 103, 106, 107, 119, 134, 138, 139, 150, 151, 156, 157, 159, 160
choice
 and meaning 9, 12, 90–91, 132–140, 151–153
 ontological 51
client-centred approach 97
co-constructed 16, 80
cognitive behavioural therapy 142
Cohn, H. 8, 15, 103
concerns, universal. *see* givens
confidentiality 25, 75
congruence 97
contract, contracting 9, 25, 26, 75–79
Cooper, M. 35, 50, 97, 120, 140, 144, 148
coping strategies 74, 122
Covid-19 156–161

d

Dasein 4, 47, 49, 148
death 4, 5, 7, 9, 10, 15, 16, 20, 22, 23, 26, 28, 31, 46, 47, 50, 51, 59, 76, 80, 86, 89, 90, 105, 107, 113, 119, 125, 128, 134, 140, 149, 154, 157, 160
denial
 disavowal 125
dependency 153
depression 34, 35, 82, 83, 106, 128, 134, 135
Descartes, R. 11
despair 4, 7, 16, 48, 52, 74, 82, 84, 111, 122, 130, 134, 148, 157
Deurzen, E. van 6, 10, 11, 16, 23, 25, 54, 59, 61, 66, 69, 92, 100, 101, 105, 107, 109, 114, 125, 134, 138, 144, 149

dialogue 12, 64, 71, 96
disclosure 101
dissociation 128–131
dread 22, 28, 82, 89, 140, 157, 158, 160
duration of therapy 25, 84

e

Eigenwelt (private world) 105, 108–110
embodiment 7, 49, 105, 143
emotions
 reflective 95, 145
 unreflective 95, 145
empathy 36, 97, 120
ending
 awareness of 15, 80
 process 26
engagement 7, 32, 83, 105, 109, 154
epoquē, *see* bracketing
equalization 60–63
existence
 Dasein 4, 47, 49, 148
 nature of 7, 23
existential anxiety
 and authenticity 82
existential approach 3, 6, 23, 31, 145
existentialists 20, 47, 48, 50, 109, 134–136, 139
existential–phenomenological theory 6
existential therapy 9, 11, 25, 37, 42, 57, 70, 91, 95, 128
existential time-limited therapy
 development 26
 ending 25–29
 expectations 23–25
 focus 21, 23, 25
 interventions 31
 limitations and possibilities 21
 model 23
 sessions 25
 structure 20

existential wheel
  centre   10
  ontic   5, 8
  ontological   5, 6
  self   5
  structure   5, 6
  time   10
expectations
  client and therapist   26
experience, subjective   4, 11, 45, 57, 58

f

facticity   7, 20, 46, 47, 50, 51, 89, 105, 138, 140, 155
fear   10, 11, 23, 24, 28–30, 50, 51, 78, 79, 82, 85–87, 89, 96, 100, 107, 117–119, 125, 129, 130, 143–145, 152–154, 158
feelings   18, 26, 28, 46, 48, 49, 60, 64, 69, 70, 74, 76–79, 82, 86, 88, 89, 94, 96, 98, 107, 108, 119, 122
felt sense   60, 89, 143, 144, 152
finitude   7, 23, 31, 90, 133, 149
focusing   66, 143, 144, 146
four worlds
  physical   105
  private   105
  social   105
  spiritual   105
frame
  cancellation policy   33
  confidentiality   25, 75
  feesm   32, 75
  negotiation of time   25, 75
framework   4, 6, 21, 30, 32, 36, 38, 47, 60, 83
Frankl, V.   134, 136, 137, 159
freedom
  of choice   51
  ontological   48–49
future   10, 15–17, 21, 30, 47, 50, 52, 86, 91, 110, 154, 157, 159, 160

g

Gendlin, E.   60, 89, 143
givens
  ontic   105
  ontological   44–52
goals or expectations   23–24
Good Faith   92, 137, 148, 150, 152

h

Heidegger, M.   4, 6–8, 15–17, 31, 43, 45–52, 69, 71, 82, 88, 92, 95, 96, 100, 105, 133, 139, 143, 148, 149, 154, 161
hermeneutics   12
horizontalisation   59, 60, 64, 65, 67
humanistic school, xiii
hum/s of existence   15
Husserl, E.   4, 11, 58, 59, 61, 69, 72

i

I-It   95, 96
imaginative variation   60, 64–67
I–Me relationship   95
inauthenticity   82, 148–150, 154
individual responses   8, 9, 11, 42, 52, 55
insecurity   5, 47, 80, 86
intentionality   11, 58, 69, 94
interconnectedness   8, 10–11, 55, 105, 143
interpretation
  descriptive   70
interventions
  associative   63–64, 68
  descriptive   70
  timing   62
isolation   4, 8, 9, 17, 55, 82, 90, 95, 107, 118, 156, 159
I-Thou   95, 97, 100

j

Jaspers, K.   51, 70, 87, 140

k

Kierkegaard, S.A. 4, 45, 49, 83, 124, 136, 148, 153

l

layers 15, 19, 41–42, 55, 83
leaping ahead 71
leaping in 71
leaves 5, 6, 8–10, 12, 20, 41–42, 54–55, 57, 74, 83, 90, 96, 110
liminal space 160
limitations
  human 138
  and possibilities 7, 113
  time 37, 145
  universal 6
listening 64, 65, 85, 98, 111, 152
Logotherapy 134
loneliness 35, 78, 90, 118, 119, 134
loss 26, 31, 71, 90, 109, 125, 130, 134, 157, 160

m

Madison, G. 143
Maslow, A. 46
May, R. 3, 4, 44, 82, 90, 104, 124, 139, 140
meaning
  and choice 13
meaninglessness 4, 9, 82, 90, 124, 132, 134, 135, 137–139
Merleau-Ponty, M. 7, 10, 45, 49, 89, 138, 140, 141, 143
Mind 6, 7, 9, 11, 12, 18, 24, 25, 32, 48, 55, 58, 59, 71, 79, 84, 88, 90, 129, 136, 140, 142, 143, 146
mind–body 11
mindfulness 60, 142–144
Mitwelt (social world) 106–107
modular approach 34–37
mood 7, 47–50, 67, 88, 98, 106, 130, 134, 143
mortality 7, 10, 28, 47, 50, 90, 155

n

National Health Service, Britain 34
neurobiology 142
neuroscience 18, 144
Nietzsche, F. W. 49, 153, 159
nothing-ness 133

o

ontic 5, 8, 10, 11, 20, 41–42, 46, 48, 50–52, 54–55, 57, 67, 74–76, 80, 82, 83, 91, 94, 96, 97, 105
ontological 41–52
ontology 4, 8
open-ended approach 26, 30, 32, 37
oughts and should 4, 148, 157

p

paradox 6, 9, 20, 75, 87, 124, 127, 133, 134, 154
past 10, 15, 16, 20, 27, 30, 46–48, 84, 110, 131, 138, 139, 154, 159
personal principles 9, 82, 113–116, 120–122, 124, 129, 131, 145, 148, 151
phenomenological 12, 57, 59
  attitude 59–60
  dance 60–69
    flow 68–69
  description 57–59
  enquiry 59, 67
phenomenology
  bracketing 61–62
  description 62
  equalization and horizontalization 62–63
  practice 63
philosophy
  Buddhism 110, 143
  Existential 3–6, 9, 20, 42, 43, 45, 65, 105, 133, 143
  phenomenology 3–13
physical world *(Umwelt)* 105

plasticity 18
polarities 9, 67, 86–87, 90, 123–131
possibilities
  and limitations 117, 151
presence 21, 47, 49, 64, 69, 97, 101, 120, 131
private world *(Eigenwelt)* 105, 108–110
psychotherapy
  application to 11–13

q

questions 4, 13, 26, 60, 61, 64–66, 69, 70, 83, 97, 99, 126, 127, 134, 138, 139, 145, 150, 158

r

Rank, O. 26, 31, 32
realms of encounter
  self-to-other 99
  self-to-self 98
  self-with-other 100–102
  self-with-world 102–103
relatedness 7, 45, 55, 59, 69–72, 94
relational self 18
relationship
  between-ness 101
  inter-relational, interpersonal 17
  I, you, we, they 94
  ontological 45–46
  presence 21, 47, 49, 64, 69, 97, 101, 120, 131
  revealing the 9, 12, 85, 93–103
  therapeutic 12, 20, 30, 31, 42, 57, 68, 95, 97, 101
resistance 70, 116
resonance 7, 11, 26, 36, 68, 70, 93, 101, 120, 143
responsibility 7, 22, 48, 52, 71, 77, 85, 91, 92, 94, 102, 117, 130, 133, 137, 139, 146, 148, 149, 152–155
Rogers, C.
  client centered 97

s

safety, safe environment 80
Sartre, J.-P. 45, 46, 48, 49, 52, 82, 87, 92, 94, 96, 97, 133, 135, 137, 138, 144, 148, 154
security 5, 46–48, 74, 86, 116, 139
sedimentation 87, 108, 115–120, 127, 128, 150, 152, 154
segments, of existential wheel 17–19
self
  plastic 18
  relational 18
  self-concept 18, 128
  self-construct 119
  self-disclosure 94
  self-esteem 13, 18, 19, 75, 108, 118, 119, 145
  self-in-process 17
  self: secure/insecure
    continuum 17–19
  self-to-other 99
  self-to-self 98
  self-with-other 100–102
self awareness
  pre-reflective 94
  reflective 94
  unreflective 94
setting 21, 23, 25, 33, 34, 52, 75, 76, 100, 105, 107, 110, 150
shoulds and oughts 4, 148, 157
social world *(Mitwelt)* 106–107
Socratic dialogue 12
somatic 85, 144
Spinelli, E. 16, 23, 47, 51, 59, 62, 70, 82, 92, 94, 97–102, 114, 116, 124, 128, 143
spirituality 134, 136
spiritual world *(Überwelt)* 105
Strasser, F. 3–161
stuck 84, 113, 115, 117, 119, 138
subjective 3–5, 11, 25, 42, 45, 52, 54, 57, 58, 64, 69, 125, 138, 143

supervision 5, 71, 80, 97, 99, 121, 157
supervisor 36
synthesis and verification 64, 66–67, 70

t

technique 61, 71–72, 103, 143
temporality 7, 10, 12, 16, 18, 21, 23, 27, 31, 47, 84
tensions in existence 124
termination 27, 32, 33, 37, 79
therapeutic relationship 12, 20, 30, 31, 42, 57, 68, 95, 97, 101
thrown-ness 46, 47, 50, 137
Tillich, P. 120, 136, 148
time
 beginnings 12
 biological time 105
 chronological 15
 circadian 105
 cultural perspective 7, 8, 34, 46, 50, 102, 109, 114
 ending 25–29
 expectations 23–25
 past, present, future 10, 15, 16, 30, 47, 154
 physical, chronological 15
 psychological 7, 57, 67, 70, 109
 revealing 85
 and temporality 10, 12, 16, 18, 23, 31, 47, 84, 105, 107, 108, 110
time, as a tool 13, 20, 21, 23
time-aware therapy 31
time constraints 159
time, cultural perspectives 7, 8, 34, 46, 50, 102, 109, 114
time-limited therapy
 approach to 30–38
 assessment 36, 37
 brief 32–33
 definition 30–31
 ending procedures 31–32
 interventions 60–64
 modular approach 34–37
 open ended 31–32
 structure 32, 34
 time-aware 32, 35
trust 28, 37, 94, 99–101, 113, 128, 129
tuning in 60, 68
tuning out 65, 67–68

u

Überwelt (spiritual world) 105
Umwelt (physical world) 105
uncertainty
 ontological 46–47
universal
 concerns 8
 givens 6–8
universalizing 6, 43
un-knowing 60, 69–72, 82, 94, 96

v

values and beliefs 24, 86, 98, 108, 124
values and patterns 83
value system 9, 18, 29, 83, 110, 119, 127, 129, 148
verb-ings 43
verification and synthesis 64, 66–67, 70

w

Warnock, M. 7
Wheel
 core 10, 14–19
 diagrams
  clarifying the worldview 9, 112–122
  discovering anxiety 9, 81–92
  establishing safety 9, 73–80
  exploring the four worlds 9, 104–111
  identifying choices 9, 132–140
  integrating mind and body 9, 141–146
 of Existence 3–13

Wheel (*cont'd*)
   ontological   46
   paradox and polarities   123–131
   phenomenological   12, 57, 59
   revealing the
     relationship   9, 93–103
   time   10, 14–19
   understanding authenticity
     9, 147–155
existential   17, 18
fulcrum   5
layers   41–42
leaves/segments   42, 54, 55, 57, 90, 110

Structure and Process, xii
world
   physical world   105
   private world   105, 108–110
   social world   106–107
   spiritual world   105
worldview
   client's   12, 13, 60, 65, 120, 122, 157
   personal   120, 124
   therapist's   37, 120–122

y

Yalom, I.   9, 23, 26, 50, 82, 90